MMXIII

THE WHITE REVIEW

EDITORS	BENJAMIN EASTHAM & JACQUES TESTARD
DESIGN, ART DIRECTION	RAY O'MEARA
POETRY EDITOR	J. S. TENNANT
ASSISTANT EDITOR	MARY HANNITY
EDITORIAL ASSISTANTS	BELLA MARRIN, OLIVER TAYLOR
READER	JEN CALLEJA
CONTRIBUTING EDITORS	JACOB BROMBERG, LAUREN ELKIN, EMMELINE FRANCIS, DANIEL MEDIN, LEE ROURKE, SAM SOLNICK, KISHANI WIDYARATNA
FUNDING & DEVELOPMENT	SOPHIE LEIGH–PEMBERTON
BOARD OF TRUSTEES	MICHAEL AMHERST, BENJAMIN EASTHAM, JACQUES TESTARD
HONORARY TRUSTEES	HANNAH BARRY, ANN & MICHAEL CAESAR, BLAINE COOK, HUGUES DE DIVONNE, TOM MORRISON–BELL, NIALL HOBHOUSE, JAMES LEIGH–PEMBERTON, MICHAEL LEUE, AMY POLLNER, PROFESSOR ANDREW PEACOCK, CÉCILE DE ROCHEQUAIRIE, HUBERT TESTARD, MICHEL TESTARD, DANIELA & RON WILLSON, CAROLINE YOUNGER

THE WHITE REVIEW IS A REGISTERED CHARITY (NUMBER 1148690)

COVER ART BY MAI-THU PERRET
PRINTED BY PUSH, LONDON
PAPER BY ANTALIS MCNAUGHTON (OLIN CREAM 100GSM, OLIN WHITE 120GSM)
BESPOKE PAPER MARBLE BY PAYHEMBURY MARBLE PAPERS
TYPESET IN JOYOUS (BLANCHE)

PUBLISHED BY THE WHITE REVIEW, MARCH 2013
EDITION OF 1,000
ISBN No. 978-0-9568001-7-6

THE WHITE REVIEW, 243 KNIGHTSBRIDGE, LONDON SW1X 7QA
WWW.THEWHITEREVIEW.ORG

EDITORIAL

A FEW ISSUES BACK we grandiosely stated 'that it is more important now than ever to provide a forum for expression and debate'. This edition of THE WHITE REVIEW goes further than its predecessors in this respect.

Come late April, the first recipient of THE WHITE REVIEW SHORT STORY PRIZE will be unveiled. Despite the number of stories still to read (it is early March, at time of writing), it is already clear that the prize has fulfilled its primary function, a forceful demonstration of the vitality of literary culture in Britain and Ireland.

This culture, and the oft-mooted notion of its decline, is the subject of a timely essay – weeks before GRANTA announces its 2013 Best of Young British Novelists' list – by Jennifer Hodgson and Patricia Waugh. 'Whatever happened to the British novel?' they ask, arguing for an alternative postwar British literary canon, and identifying the current 'British literary establishment' as 'the perfect pricks, so to speak, to kick against'.

Also, provocatively, in this issue: a GUARDIAN reader critiques its opinion pages; and Keston Sutherland, interviewed, asserts the ability of radical poetry to effect the 'fundamental transformation of human life'. Really touchy readers might even take exception to Lawrence Lek's wonderfully esoteric take on the Shard, 'the last building of the twentieth century'.

Those habitually drawn to THE WHITE REVIEW for fiction, art or poetry should not shun us in favour of less essayistic climes. This issue sees us renewing our commitment to fiction and poetry in translation – with new work by Edouard Levé (conceptual art meets Oulipo), Peter Stamm and the venerable Yves Bonnefoy – and to new writers such as Jesse Loncraine. Luc Tuymans and John Stezaker, finally, complete our trio of interviews, artworlds apart, diametrically opposed in their conceptions of the artistic process. Both contribute a series of images, as does artist-photographer Talia Chetrit.

If pressed, we might say this was our best issue yet. We hope you agree.

THE EDITORS

CONTENTS

Cover:
UNTITLED by MAI–THU PERRET
Courtesy of Collection of Vidya Gastaldon, France
Photo by Annik Wetter, Geneva

PAGE INDEX:
{ A—Art, F—Fiction, E—Essay, P—Poetry }

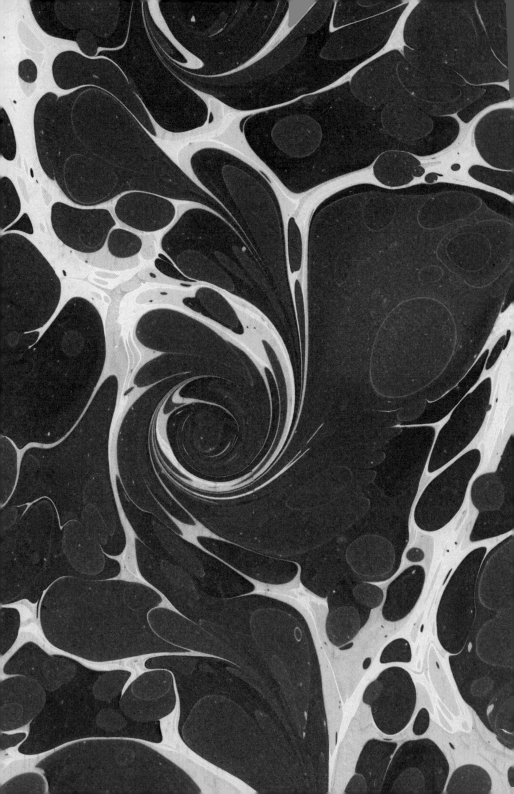

ŒUVRES

BY

EDOUARD LEVÉ

(*tr.* JAN STEYN)

1. A book describes works conceived but not realised by the author.

2. The world is drawn from memory. There are missing countries, altered borders.

3. Proust's head is drawn on a page of *À LA RECHERCHE DU TEMPS PERDU*. The words that trace out the contour of his face form a grammatically correct sentence.

4. Man-sized aluminium mannequins are dropped at different heights from a crane. Metamorphosed by folds, they adopt the pose to which they are constrained by their new morphology.

5. An exhibit displays pieces unalike in spirit, style and technique, but with the same origin: their author saw them while dreaming.

6. Entomological boxes contain invitation cards to exhibitions that did not take place. The reasons for their cancellation are written below the cards. The boxes are hung on the walls like a collection of insects.

7. A woman's voice describes the shapes she sees in the static snow on the television screen after the end of broadcasts. Geometric forms, windmills, ghosts. The video is shown on a monitor posed on a low table at the foot of a divan couch. The visitor lies down and compares what he sees to what he hears.

8. *MUSEUM OF NOBODIES*. Instead of the usual celebrities, a wax museum presents unknown characters. Chosen at random from the telephone book, the models are representative of neither an epoch, nor a region, nor a profession. At its inauguration the museum shows thirty statues. Two new models are added to the museum's collection each year: as the years go by an evolving, sculptural and hyperrealist memory of society emerges.

9. Every year in January a painting is made from memory of the same photograph, which represents a square in Bangkok during a time of affluence. Neither the model image, nor the preceding paintings are looked at. After ten years the paintings are revealed and exhibited alongside one another.

10. A scene of a film is shown backwards to actors so they can learn to act it out in reverse. Once they succeed, they are filmed anew. The new scene, in turn projected backwards, becomes strange: reversing the inversion doesn't get you back to where you started.

11. The friend of an artist selects descriptions of artworks from press reviews of exhibitions. The accompanying photograph is cut out and the text sent to the artist to draw the work based on its description. The final work is a triptych composed of the drawing, the description of the work and the photograph accompanying the article. There are four authors, direct or indirect, voluntary or involuntary: the artist who created the referenced work, the writer of the article, the friend who chose it, and the artist who drew it.

12. A scene reflected in the retina of an eye. Photograph.

13. A sculpture represents a man whose extremities, instead of jutting out, extend into the interior of his body. The head, hands, feet and sex are folded in. The man sits on the ground, legs spread and arms folded. Marble.

14. The floor of a cage is littered with pages from the Old Testament. For a month, a record is kept of the words upon which a hummingbird comes to rest. A text is written using only these words.

15. A leather jacket made from a mad cow.

16. A hundred pictorial or sculptural representations of a biblical character, from different times and countries, are photographed using the same framing. A print is made by superimposing the negatives. Appearing in a halo are the average faces of Adam, Eve, Mary, Jesus, and God.

17. A litre of molten lead is poured out in zero gravity in a vacuum. Brought back to earth, they are exposed in the form into which they have hardened.

18. *The Mimic*. In a yellow hall lit in yellow light, the voice of an artist is heard telling his life story in the form of an anamnesis, from his birth right up to the day of the exhibition. The voice is not his, but that of a professional mimic. Yet nothing gives this away.

19. A butterfly is released into a room that cannot be seen. Every night, its flight, detected by laser beams, is transmitted to a mobile machine equipped with a leaky hourglass. By morning, the imprint of the nocturnal flight is drawn in sand on the floor.

20. In the United States a voyage is undertaken to photograph towns with names

that are homonyms of towns in other countries. The itinerary, which connects
them by passing only once through each town, goes around the country in thirteen
thousand kilometres. The trajectory commences in New York, follows the coast
to the South, heads West up to the Pacific, climbs back up North, and follows the
Canadian border to the North–East before returning to the starting point. The route
is traversed by car. The towns crossed are, in alphabetic order:

AMSTERDAM, BAGDAD, BELFAST, BELGRADE, BELLEVILLE,
BERLIN, BETHLEHEM, BETHUNE, BRISTOL, CALAIS, CAMBRIDGE,
CANTON, CARLSBAD, CARTHAGE, CLERMONT, CUBA, DELHI,
DUBLIN, FLORENCE, FRANKFORT, GLASGOW, HEIDELBERG,
JERICHO, JOHANNESBURG, LIMA, LIVERPOOL, MACON, MADRAS,
MADRID, MANCHESTER, MELBOURNE, MEXICO, MILAN, MILO,
MONTEVIDEO, NAPLES, ODESSA, OXFORD, PANAMA, PARIS,
PEKING, POTSDAM, ROME, ROTTERDAM, SAINT–CLOUD, SEVILLE,
STOCKHOLM, STUTTGART, SYRACUSE, TORONTO, TOULON,
VERSAILLES.

In these towns photographs are taken of common places, in the double sense
of banal places and places where the community gathers. Each photograph is
accompanied by a title: CUBA'S TOWN HALL; A BAR IN BERLIN; SUPERMARKET IN
ROME; HAIRDRESSING SALON IN PARIS; A STREET IN VERSAILLES. Descriptions that
are misleading without being false.

21. A pillow is filled with feathers lost by birds at the moment of taking flight.
On the white pillowcase is embroidered: 'Flythms'.

22. Paintings combining contradictory techniques, formats, styles, or modes of
presentation. A grey monochrome in a gilded baroque frame. A geometric painting
with matter–painting impastos. A large–scale miniature. A Chinese scroll depicting
Paris. A blurry hyperrealist picture. A pop art portrait of the cardinal de Retz.

23. During a film shoot, the actors don't open their mouths, but inwardly speak their
lines. They are then dubbed using their own voices. Though synchronic, the sound
and image remain dissociated.

24. A house designed by a 3–year–old is built.

25. A lunette before a window, inside an exhibition space situated on an overhang, allows one to see works installed in a village a few kilometres away in the background. Their placement (in gardens, on rooftops, behind walls) makes the works invisible from the village itself.

26. A building is transformed into a cemetery. The rooms become vaults.

27. Cello pieces written by amateurs, with the aid of an arranger and a cellist. The former musically translates suggestions by the amateur, which the latter plays for him to judge and correct. A professional soloist plays the finished pieces. A record is released.

28. The number of works in a museum is added to without the knowledge of its employees. False modern and contemporary pieces, or ones that are authentic and donated by living artists in on the ruse, are deposited in the storerooms. Three people make appointments with a curator to consult artworks kept there. While two of them distract the curator, the third plants a small parasitic piece in the collection.

29. A picture is painted. A detail, copied onto another canvas, acts as a point of departure for a second picture. A detail, copied from the second picture, different to the preceding one, is copied onto a third canvas, on which another picture takes shape around it. And so on. The series is a chain of which the pictures are the links, and the details the points where they meet.

30. A house is built without the use of measurement. Each measure is intuitively estimated. The materials are contemporary and the banal style is that of mass-produced houses. At first blush, the house seems normal. Looking closer, one sees numerous errors. The partitions are poorly joined. The steps are poorly assembled. The flagstones are not parallel to the walls. These, along with the windows and the doors, are not set square. The roof is not watertight.

31. *VETERANS OF JOY*. Aged hedonists, men and women more than 60 years old, are photographed in their homes. Old rock stars, clubbers, demimondaines, swingers, porn stars.

32. The user's instructions of a piece of translation software is subjected to translation, twice, by the same software, from a foreign language and back again. The work consists of a copy of the original instructions alongside the different enough, doubly translated text.

33. The noises heard in a landscape are written on the walls and floor of a room. The size of the lettering is proportional to the intensity and distance of their sounds. Their position on the wall corresponds to where they appear in the landscape.

'Crickets
Slow shrill birdsong
The buzz of a fly
Children playing in the distance
Bird whistling, several shrill notes
Bird shrieking, tapering off
Children speaking in the distance
Crickets
Shrill bird whistle
An adult addressing the children in the distance
Slide of a ballpoint pen over a sheet of paper
The moo of a cow
Shrill bird
Buzz of a fly, it comes to rest, its legs knocking against the plastic table
Flight of a bumblebee
Scratching of my nails on my shoulders
I sniff
I breathe
Shrill bird
Cuckoo
I swallow
I move the notebook, scraping against the plastic table
Airplane far off
Wasps around the nest they're building
Fly on my left arm
I chase it off: the bones in my shoulders creak
Telephone.'

34. The hanging of a museum's permanent collection is changed for the duration of an exhibit. The choice of works remains the same, but the order of their appearance in the flow of halls changes. They are ordered by decreasing size.

35. Fake drawings by artists from the early twentieth century are folded up and inserted into books in provincial libraries. The books are chosen for the coincidence of their dates of publication and the supposed dates of the drawings. At an undetermined date, a reader discovers the work. Not imagining that it might be a fake, since the normal motive for forgery – the pecuniary enrichment of the forger – is not operative here, experts authenticate the drawing. The artist's body of works is augmented. Wrongly so.

36. Music for a single instrument is written by transcribing texts into musical scores. For each letter there is a corresponding note. The spaces between words mark rests. The choice of notes corresponding to letters determines the tune.

37. A photograph of a man's face is cut down the middle from top to bottom. One half is kept protected from the light. The other is taped to the man's place of residence, exposed to the sun and elements. One year later, the photograph is reconstituted by reassembling the two pieces.

38. An artist is filmed under hypnosis. The videotape shows the beginning of the session, the wait, and then his passage into a hypnotic state. The hypnotist's voice accompanies the images. His awakening is not recorded. Watching the video plunges the artist back into a state of hypnosis which only the hypnotist can bring him out of. The hypnotist having disappeared, the artist cannot take the risk of watching the tape. Having chosen to show it, he is the only one who cannot watch it.

[This is an extract from *Œuvres*, to be published in early 2014 by Dalkey Archive Press.]

COMMENT IS FRAUGHT: A POLEMIC

BY

MR GUARDIANISTA

WHEN NOT LISTENING to the phone messages of recently deceased children or smearing those killed in stadium disasters, journalists at Britain's largest-selling newspaper, the *SUN*, may find time to pen light-hearted satires of modern life. One such piece was published in January 2003, depicting a new cast of 'Mr Men' characters that best reflect twenty-first century Britain. After a handful of readers went to the Press Complaints Commission, failing to see the funny side to 'Mr Asylum Seeker', 'Mr Yardie', and 'Mr Albanian Gangster', a new figure was created just for them, 'Mr Guardianista':

> He suffers bouts of guilt about the poor and homeless but tries not to let it spoil his holiday at a gîte in Provence. Dare support the toppling of Saddam Hussein and he'll choke on his organic vegetarian lunch (washed down with a subtle Chilean chardonnay). Mr Guardianista is also likely to be a student well after an age when he should be working for a living and contributing to a society he thinks owes him one.

GUARDIAN readers like myself expect, and embrace, such attacks – we are amazed that our dwindling band of Guardianistas continues to occupy such a prominent place in the national mindset. Only 200,000 of us are willing to pay £1.40 (£2.30 on Saturday) for the paper, a drop of 11 per cent from last year. Guardian.co.uk may attract over four million unique hits a day (second only to Mail Online in the UK), but the *GUARDIAN*'s print readership is just over a tenth of the *DAILY MAIL*'s and half that of *THE TIMES*. More Britons buy the *SCOTTISH DAILY RECORD*, yet (as far as I am aware) no pejorative term exists for its patrons.

 GUARDIAN staff members have enough self-awareness to understand that their work is not to everyone's taste. Last year Michael White, the paper's assistant editor, listed the charge sheet as follows: 'Naive, subversive, priggish, lentil-eating, sandal-wearing, feminist, humourless.' Outside of the fold, cartoonish reactionaries tend to project their personal anxieties onto the paper, failing to step back and acknowledge their own ridiculousness. Richard Littlejohn, author of *LITTLEJOHN'S BRITAIN* and former presenter of Sky News's *LITTLEJOHN*, finds Guardianistas 'self-regarding'. Seemingly still fighting the Cold War, the former Conservative Defence Minister Sir Gerald Howarth believes it to be a 'communist newspaper'.

 Calmer criticism of the paper tends to point to two areas of dispute. Firstly, that it is a loss-making enterprise (last year Guardian Media Group reported an annual loss of £76 million) with plummeting circulation – surely an issue afflicting every major news publisher to varying degrees as the British press continues to haemorrhage readers. Secondly, that it is hypocritical for publishing editorial commentary damning big business, while accepting corporate advertising revenue and relying on private equity to survive. The owners, Scott Trust Limited, clearly believe that to function as an influential 'mainstream' publication, they must take the corporate shilling whilst ensuring that 'the journalistic freedom and liberal values of the *GUARDIAN*' are safe-guarded. Their paper is up against nine other national dailies, none noticeably 'moral' in this regard, and only one (the *INDEPENDENT*) could claim to hold a similar 'liberal' outlook.

❡ The *GUARDIAN*'s perspective is shaped by its history. Emerging from the aftermath of the Peterloo massacre of pro-democracy demonstrators in Manchester, the first issue was printed from an office under a cutler's shop on 5 May 1821. Under the stewardship of a politically active local cotton merchant, John Edward Taylor, the weekly *MANCHESTER GUARDIAN* demonstrated an Enlightenment inheritance, seeking to 'zealously enforce the principles of civil and religious Liberty'. The paper would eschew provinciality and embrace political culture beyond Britain's borders, enchanted by the 'magnificent experiments' taking place across nineteenth-century Europe and Latin America 'to replace antiquated and despotic Governments'.

Published daily from 1855, the broadsheet grew in influence during the renowned 57-year editorship of Charles Prestwich Scott (1872-1929). Scott believed that the values of 'honesty, cleanness, courage, fairness, a sense of duty to the reader and the community' informed the character of his newspaper. Moving print operations to London in the early 1960s, the paper managed to keep a foot in the civil society movement as one of the few established outlets acknowledging human rights activism – a rare national voice in solidarity with women, disabled people, ethnic minorities, gay people (not to mention trade unionists and public sector workers) across Britain. Occasionally supportive of an emerging 'counterculture', the *GUARDIAN* was better able than its rivals to establish a young readership base – over half of readers in 1981 were under 35.

To this day, the *GUARDIAN* portrays itself as youthful and radical compared to its competitors, laying siege to traditional institutions and slaying sacred cows. Indeed, the paper's most celebrated interventions have often agitated establishment figures – from its public reservations around military action in Suez, the Falklands and Iraq, to exposing Tory 'sleaze' during the Major years, up to the recent publication of US diplomatic cables obtained by WikiLeaks and challenging Rupert Murdoch over the phone-hacking scandal.

Of course, the *GUARDIAN* has never been 'anti-establishment'. Its editors have cultivated warm friendships with prime ministers – C. P. Scott with the Liberal Party's David Lloyd George, Alastair Hetherington (editor from 1956-75) with Labour's Harold Wilson. Conservative PM Ted Heath, accompanied by Federal German Chancellor Willy Brandt, was guest of honour at the black-tie dinner celebrating the *GUARDIAN*'s 150th anniversary. The nineties saw disgruntled former contributors

E

make their frustrations known about the paper's devotion to New Labour. Mark Steel wrote that when his contract expired he was told the paper would 'realign towards Tony Blair'. Will Self continued the theme, saying that when he left the stable, it was 'little more than the lickspittle house journal of New Labour. The GUARDIAN is now a tabloid-broadsheet, a DAILY MAIL for the dumbed-down and deracinated.'

Insights into this relationship between *progressive* government and *progressive* newspaper appear throughout the 'off-the-record' notes meticulously kept by Hugo Young, the GUARDIAN's senior political commentator until his death in 2003. One such recollection from 2001 features then-Chancellor Gordon Brown extending a breakfast invitation to Young and senior members of the GUARDIAN team (including editor Alan Rusbridger, Polly Toynbee, Larry Elliott, Martin Kettle and Michael White – all remain at the paper). 'Mainly a virtuoso performance from GB to persuade us of the need to join in the great campaign to argue more for public investment,' Young writes. 'We, the GUARDIAN, had written big pieces about this for some time ... and now we needed to get behind the government (he implied) in proposing much more spending.' Aware of the intimacy, Young further notes that some had taken to terming his employer 'the Gordian'.

This attachment, however, did not jeopardise the paper's relations with the political Right. Prime Minister David Cameron – who as a lowly parliamentary candidate began a fortnightly diary column for the GUARDIAN until 2004 – has enjoyed occasional meetings with the current editor, and even appointed a former GUARDIAN columnist and leader writer, Julian Glover, as his chief speechwriter in 2011. Past editors at leading Conservative newspapers – Geoffrey Wheatcroft, Sir Simon Jenkins and Sir Max Hastings – found a new lease of life in the new century after being handed their own weekly columns. 'I write for the GUARDIAN,' Hastings commented in 2005, 'because it is read by the new establishment.'

❡ Central to the GUARDIAN's ethos are its editorial columns. The paper has long been admired for its opinion pages. As Scott declared, 'The voice of opponents no less than that of friends has a right to be heard.' Brendan Bracken, Winston Churchill's wartime Minister of Information, praised the GUARDIAN to a group of newspaper editors, saying: 'Some people call it the greatest newspaper in the world. I have always called it the greatest viewspaper in the world.'

Columnist Seumas Milne, who was comment editor from 2001 to 2007, argues that the breadth of commentary in his pages was unrivalled in global media during the immediate aftermath of 9/11. '[The GUARDIAN's] comment pages hosted the full range of views the bulk of the media blanked; in other words, the paper gave rein to the pluralism that most media gatekeepers claim to favour in principle, but struggle to put into practice.' His paper certainly goes further than its rivals to promote diversity of political opinion. A spirit of inclusivity sees politicians of every stripe, 'experts', activists, public figures and thinkers from Left to Right offered the opportunity to remark upon the news agenda. The comment pages have opened up and the *GUARDIAN* reader is now able to read occasional political opinions from radical Marxists or right-wing outliers. Commentary from abroad, notably through the expansion of its online Comment is Free section, includes anti-imperialists and senior Bush-era apparatchiks, and encourages perspectives from non-Anglophone commentators – a rare assortment among the British media.

But it is the regular stall of heavily-promoted writers, the unrelenting main-stays whose weekly contributions are fixtures within the comment pages, who are inseparable from Brand Guardian. An 'editorial line' is almost impossible to define accurately: as long-time political columnist Jackie Ashley noted in 2008, the *GUARDIAN* 'isn't a single file of believers marching in step', though she adds that 'it is clearly left-of-centre and vaguely progressive'. Its columnists and their counterparts at rival national dailies have cultivated an informed political consensus – they derive their authority not from any expertise or unique insight into political affairs, rather from their willingness to consistently comment on them. They remain unfazed by events – always eager to express their opinions.

The *GUARDIAN* certainly prides its prize political pundits – most have been working for the paper for at least a decade and show little sign of moving on. Not only do they perform the valuable function of contributing regular content at a time when resources for gathering news are scarce. They act as its representatives on earth, missionaries visiting broadcast studios across the world, extending its reach by preaching the *GUARDIAN*'s gospel to unconverted audiences.

Is the paper's pride misplaced?

¶ Newspaper columnists in the 'prestige press' do not provide a public service. They are not balanced, neutral or objective. They do not seek to break stories, uncover misdeeds or unravel conspiracy. They are given weekly slots to impart instant judgments on matters deemed 'newsworthy' at any given time. The same 'Big Issues' have been raked over for decades now: Britain in Europe, the public/state school divide, privatising the public sector, support for American foreign policy objectives, voting reform, criminal justice: to punish or rehabilitate? These topics have been discussed for so long that a sense of ennui has set in – the 'agenda-setting' commentator has nothing new to say.

Take Timothy Garton Ash, Oxford Professor, advisor and friend to world states-men, who has been writing a weekly *GUARDIAN* column since 2004. A change at the Elysée Palace will prompt him to call for an 'Entente Cordiale' between Britain and France. Reacting to events, he may challenge the prime minister to bolster Britain's relationship with the EU, or declare that Scotland should not leave the United Kingdom. He might warn of external threats – from Russia, China, the Middle East. Occasionally, he goes out on a limb, encouraging Europeans to sing the same anthem, or speak a common language.

Using hackneyed metaphors (Europe is a car with 'Germany in the driving seat' and France in 'the front passenger seat') and inelegant attempts at humour (Sarkozy shouting, '*Non, non, ma chérie! Tout droit, tout droit!*' in the aforementioned 'vehicle'), Garton Ash's column depicts a world far removed from reality. 'Come on, India!' he hollers, ensuring that he has made the obligatory references to Bollywood and cricket before addressing the country of 1.2 billion people, 'start beating China at politics.' Writing as if complexity would frighten his readers, he has individuals exemplifying diverse nations, and nations embodying ideals: 'Britain has become more Swiss, but most of Europe's gone German.'

In the world of Timothy Garton Ash and his colleagues, politics must be simplified for the audience, and the subjects given prominent editorial space are disparate and highly selective. The regular GUARDIAN columnist is on a perpetual cycle, always at hand to provide the continuation of on–going 'stories'. They are afflicted by schizophrenic short–term moralism – the reader is given the impression that an issue is of urgent concern, only to be forgotten soon after. We are goaded into feeling guilty for a week, about poor kids, the Eurozone, the forest sell–off, sexual violence, farm–workers' wages. Then we are ushered along, the unsolved dilemmas building up behind us.

Rarely exceeding readers' expectations, the commentariat barks out its opinions against any particular backdrop. The London Olympics gifted Polly Toynbee four pieces in four weeks to illustrate her political positions on disability benefits, growing inequality levels, school sport and postwar British history. Jackie Ashley uses the Olympics more sparingly: Beijing 2008 had something to say about obesity; London 2012 represented 'hard work', 'sacrifice' and a 'sense of belonging'.

Concerns come into view only to disappear. Events elicit the same predictable reactions. The Queen's Diamond Jubilee, for example, allowed Sir Simon Jenkins to exhibit his monarchist credentials ('Sit back, relax and enjoy it'), which were similarly on display for the Royal Wedding the previous year ('Just relax and enjoy the fun'). This purely reactive commentary, addressing issues fleetingly and in isolation, does little to contribute to a growing understanding of the public sphere, leaving real and rhetorical shifts undetected, and readers uninformed.

❡ The late historian Tony Judt believed that certain liberal intellectuals were 'familiar – and comfortable – with a binary division of the world along ideological lines', confident in asserting their 'monopoly of insight into world affairs'. The impression their audiences are left with is that a grand struggle is taking place which is to be won or lost.

This worldview encourages the GUARDIAN columnist to brandish their tribal loyalty at every opportunity and rally against the enemies of progress. The opposition is varied and ill-defined – it could be the 'ConDem' government; malicious corp-orations; the American hegemon. This binary division is a throwback to an era of mass parties, when there were two distinct positions in British political life, aligned with popular movements. It is tempting to seek a return to simpler political times, by drawing out clear dividing lines, lauding your side while reviling the other.

Readers are offered the chance to delegate responsibility onto these partisan writers. Audiences are armed with handy cut-out-and-keep arguments explaining why we should all jump aboard the bandwagon, lest we are left behind. Hopes and ambitions are pinned onto parties, factions, individuals; fears and anxieties are projected onto their rivals. We are encouraged to put any deep analysis on hold: as long as we pick the right side, we are told, we will be alright.

'If there is one thing we still do really well in the media,' declared Jackie Ashley in a moment of self-acknowledgement, 'it's losing our heads.' A GUARDIAN columnist for over a decade now, Ashley lives and breathes Labour politics. Her father was an MP for the party for twenty-six years and a peer for twenty more, whilst she cut her teeth in print journalism as the political editor of the Labour-backed NEW STATESMAN. Yet she understands the party in terms of personality rather than policy – in awe of reputations, only to have her head turned by the next big thing. Having spent years arguing that Gordon Brown was 'needed in No 10' and publishing frequent 'Blair must go' columns, Ashley eventually grew weary. 'Tony Blair should not quit. And things are actually going rather well for Labour,' she insisted in February 2007.

When he stepped down just a few months later and Brown assumed office, Ashley proclaimed that 'we are in a new phase, far more energetic and interesting than the doldrums of recent months'. Gordon was 'fast, agile, ruthless' – his tenure would be 'a Tory nightmare'. This feeling was short-lived: by Christmas, the party had 'lost its way' and in August 2008 she believed that the 'best thing would be for him to stand aside', (for David Miliband as it happens), 'with a rueful smile and a few blunt words of regret'. The next month she changed her mind, following a conference speech that she felt was 'good enough for those who have written off the prime minister'. Ashley ended up voting Liberal Democrat in 2010 after doing a 'vote-swap' with a friend from Streatham.

For the commentariat, politics is reduced to taking sides. *Who do you 'support'? Whose 'team' are you on? Are you with us or against us?* Yet what does pledging your support mean if it does nothing to effect positive change on the ground? It simply makes the 'supporter' feel better. Ignorant about consequences, at least they are happy in the knowledge that they backed the right side.

❡ Is the power of the press over society exaggerated? The GUARDIAN's media guru
Roy Greenslade believes that it certainly plays a role in shaping public opinion. He
writes: 'The newspapers' daily drip–drip–drip of stories and commentaries – whether
positive or negative – do influence the electorate, including those people who never
read the papers. The repetition, and the influence over other media, are the key to
creating a broad consensus.'

Influencing opinion is one thing – instigating action is another. The GUARDIAN's
occasional direct interventions have been somewhat ill-fated. In 2004, with the US
presidential election looming, the paper believed that it could apply pressure on
President George W. Bush from across the pond. Members of the editorial team
initiated a letter–writing campaign to undecided voters in a marginal county within
the crucial swing state of Ohio. Armed with advice such as 'handwrite your letter,
for additional impact', and tempted by the promise of free flights for the best–written
letters, 14,000 readers signed up to correspond with the residents of Clark County.

The strategy provoked an unexpected reaction. Rush Limbaugh, Fox News
and Republican net warriors used the campaign to rabble–rouse for Bush against
Democratic challenger John Kerry, leading to an 'unprecedented email bombardment'
of the GUARDIAN's newsdesk. The largely negative responses ranged from abusive
('Each email someone gets from some arrogant Brit telling us why to NOT vote for
George Bush is going to backfire, you stupid, yellow–toothed pansies'); to disappointed
('Nothing will do more to undermine the Democratic cause in Ohio'); and sarcastic
('I am barely literate, so please don't use big, fancy words. Set me straight, folks!').

Operation Clark County was soon aborted. But the paper had been prescient in
its decision to target Ohio – after a closely fought campaign, the state's electors may
have decided the presidency. As the US magazine SLATE noted after the election, of
the sixteen districts Al Gore won in 2000, Kerry won them all except Clark County.
'In 2000, Al Gore won Clark County by 324 votes ... On Tuesday George Bush
won Clark County by 1,620 votes.' The magazine quoted the GUARDIAN's Ian Katz
(then editor of the paper's weekday supplement, G2) as saying that it would be 'self–
aggrandising' to claim that the paper's operation affected the election result. 'Don't be
so modest, Ian,' came the retort.

Whether it is launching bewildering initiatives in order to affect overseas
elections, or at home encouraging readers to vote Liberal Democrat in 2010 'to prevent
a Conservative win', the GUARDIAN has often displayed an inability to critically
scrutinise complex events and their after–effects. The paper demonstrates a passion
for political affairs, yet its editors rarely have a special insight into consequences.

Journalism is prone to simplification. The sprawling, multi–faceted nature of

E

politics cannot be reduced to a series of tick-boxes – 'Five ways to solve the Eurozone crisis'; 'Eight steps to make Britain a fair society'; 'Five ways Labour can fight back'. Just as reactionaries need an imagined past to orientate themselves, GUARDIAN liberals have faith in an idealised future. But they fail to offer a coherent, pluralistic vision of a just society – we are simply assured that things will be better if only we would heed their sage advice.

Vagueness masks ignorance. We cannot end child poverty at the snap of our fingers, or CLICK HERE to stop sexual violence. Columnists covering these subjects may hint at a problem, but are only fractionally more incisive than those cartoons in the OBSERVER of a loosely-shackled, slobbering bear with 'Financial Markets' emblazoned across its chest, or a Fat Cat (literally a 'fat cat') smoking a cigar whilst a bare-buttocked George Osborne smirks inanely in the background. This hollowed-out critical thinking ensures a personal compliance with an increasingly lost and profoundly confused political landscape. It is difficult to come to terms with the fact that there may not be easy-to-digest, practical 'solutions' to political problems.

¶ For the GUARDIAN writer, events don't really happen unless they are 'evaluated'. The reader is brusquely told of an event's significance rather than offered time to formulate his or her own opinions. And rather than adequately reflecting common experience, the writer's column may become a refuge from reality.

2 October, 2012: The leader of the opposition delivers a co-written, pre-planned mid-term conference speech to party supporters on a Tuesday afternoon in a hall in Manchester. Key sections are trailed beforehand in the day's newspapers and it is finally streamed to a television audience smaller than that afternoon's edition of the quiz show COUNTDOWN.

The following morning, Polly Toynbee was on hand to tell us the meaning of this particular 'event'. Taking to the GUARDIAN's front page, she proclaimed 'the day Ed Miliband wiped the smile off Conservative faces' as 'breathtaking', noting the 'warmth of spontaneous affection' that his rapt audience displayed. Adopting the role of interpreter, she declared: 'This was the day Miliband took full command of his party and turned his private qualities at last into public strengths.' If readers were in any doubt about the importance of this performance, we were assured that 'by osmosis voters do absorb political turning points such as this'.

Who is this 'expert on the present' trying to persuade? And why is she mystifying her audience by taking control of the narrative? Is her audience of potential 'voters' not capable of deciding what counts as a 'turning point' or what can be considered a *public* strength?

Polly Toynbee, the GUARDIAN made flesh to many observers, has her detractors throughout the conservative commentariat. Mayor of London Boris Johnson wrote in the DAILY TELEGRAPH that she 'incarnates all the nannying, high-taxing, high-spending schoolmarminess of Blair's Britain'. DAILY MAIL writers have described 'the GUARDIAN's high-priestess' as 'snooty' and 'hectoring'. But must GUARDIAN readers rally to her defence in the face of hostility? Behind the invective sadly lies a kernel of truth. Toynbee adopts a prescriptive tone not only alienating to the right-wing press, but more importantly to the people she believes she is supporting.

At the end of last year, she used her column to invoke the plight of disadvantaged people across the UK, yet could only view their situations through the lens of party politics. Lazy proclamations such as 'Labour would certainly rebalance the burden of hardship as best it could', or about 'key voters who feel the cut painfully and who take offence at Tory stigmatisation' make it seem like the deprived have been recruited to back her party political positions.

Newspaper columnists often believe they are entitled to use the spectre of 'the public' to support their arguments whilst simultaneously denying them a direct voice. That poor people are poor is of interest to the commentator, but she remains averse to their active participation in media discourse. The views of *ordinary* people are delegitimised – their perspectives rejected through spatial constraints, unless reduced to a (very occasional) trite soundbite: 'There's just no work for the young,' a Hackney headmaster was briefly quoted as saying by Toynbee, fumbling for an explanation for the 2011 summer riots.

But surely we need visible progressive champions fighting for the marginalised while the forces of reaction dominate the media landscape? Writers like Toynbee, who have 'an instinctive defence of the underdog against the over-privileged, rooting for the have-nots against the power of the have-yachts', must play a key role in balancing out the shrill voices demonising the dispossessed.

Those who take this view understand political commentary as both adversarial and elitist – the writers on either side privilege themselves, certain of their own centrality to debates. They see a split between 'Bad' people calling for a continuation of suffering and misery, and the 'Good' defenders of decency. But both 'Bad' and 'Good' share the view that it is *they* that know best – it is naturally up to *them* to decide what must be done.

Invariably, this plays a role in silencing the public who, it seems, exist only to be talked about or analysed by media folk, according to what comes into view. Those who are talked about are denied direct access to the media, their voices excluded from the debate. Disconnected, we get to hear about gender inequality because some female journalists have garnered misogynistic comments on Twitter; discuss race because a black player has been verbally abused at a football match; mention disablism because the Paralympics is on.

Real life human experiences are only to be seen through the extraordinarily narrow prism of media interest. As Polly predicts for 2013, 'Expect shocking stories of families losing children's disability living allowance. Picture disabled people chaining themselves to mobility scooters about to be repossessed.' That's one less illustrated opinion page to plan for the coming year.

❡ The *GUARDIAN* has a proud history of being underestimated by its rivals when taking an independent line. It has provoked premature obituaries, as it did in the early 1960s when the paper questioned the press's conduct in hounding a junior minister, Thomas Galbraith, following a 'scurrilous' campaign to link him with a Russian spy. 'The *GUARDIAN* was a magnificent newspaper, vibrant in ideas and originality, swift and sure-footed in leadership,' an editorial in the *MIRROR* read, after Galbraith's resignation. 'It has swapped its majestic virtues for vacillation and timidity ... Worse a smugness has settled around it thicker than a London (or Manchester) fog.'

Half a century later, and many of the *GUARDIAN*'s opponents disparaged the paper in the wake of the hacking scandal. The *SUN* published frequent commentary arguing that claims were baseless; Boris Johnson believed them to be 'codswallop', 'politically motivated'. Yet the paper helped to cease the publication of the 168-year old *NEWS OF THE WORLD* – forced to say farewell to its '7.5 million loyal readers' – and precipitate the departure of several senior executives at Rupert Murdoch's multinational News Corporation.

According to editor Alan Rusbridger, the *GUARDIAN* has 'always been an outsider. It's never been in the club.' Well, if he's not in the club, must he still play by club rules? Do the 'culture, practices and ethics of the press' (the Leveson Inquiry's remit) even matter now that the era of 'the press' is over? Rusbridger seeks a foothold in the future, an innovative, 'digital-first' future beyond print. And as his paper takes its leap into the unknown, its brand is strong – far stronger than its larger UK print rivals dwarfing his paper's circulation.

Editorially, the *GUARDIAN* is almost alone in commissioning world leaders, Nobel Prize-winning economists, radical academics and human rights activists who can offer up their knowledge and expertise to anyone with an internet connection, free of charge. Many are still forced to self-censor, whipping up narrow articles devoid of context, meticulously sticking to word-counts and wildly acknowledging passing fads: 'What "Gangnam Style" says about Asian identity'; '*ZERO DARK THIRTY* and the normalisation of torture'; 'Mayan Apocalypse, meet Fiscal Cliff'. There is little room for the myriad experiences of those historically excluded from the media arena.

There is no need for spatial or thematic constraints in the digital future. The *GUARDIAN* is in a position to decide whether it wants to emerge as an influential educative force, an honest voice for its growing, diverse readership, intelligent enough to come to its own conclusions if presented with reliable information. Or does it want

E

to operate as the 'better' part of an industry indifferent to positive world change?

The GUARDIAN can survive without its canon of consistent commentators. They are an anachronism – talking about everything yet saying nothing. Cancel their contracts and help break their tedious cycle of responses. Broaden the comment base to enrich the discourse. Move beyond a reactive, adversarial approach and offer up space to help readers connect with the political world in all its complexity and contradictions. Or, failing that, stick 'The Talent' behind a paywall and let them sing for their supper. They can do their shouting in the dark, at those with more money than sense.

We won't miss them.

INTERVIEW

WITH

LUC TUYMANS

LUC TUYMANS IS CONSIDERED ONE OF THE GREATEST PAINTERS WORKING TODAY – quantified by the demand for and prices of his works, and the over one hundred solo shows he has opened; and qualified by his near-unanimous popularity within the usually hypercritical artworld. He has been characterised as a reductive painter – because of his very subtle colour palette and precisely fuzzy lines – a minimalist, a definitively European painter, a postmodern history painter, and the list goes on. But he'll have none of it: Tuymans eschews all categories, vocally and with borderline disgust.

I met with him in early January, on the eve of the opening of *THE SUMMER IS OVER* at David Zwirner Gallery in New York – his tenth exhibition since joining the gallery in 1994. Though it was initially set to open in early November, the show was postponed when Hurricane Sandy ripped through the north-eastern United States, devastating the Chelsea art district. Much of the Hudson River-facing neighbourhood was under water. Tuymans had started to install the show when the storm hit, and post-Sandy he found his paintings floating on four feet of seawater that had pushed its way beyond the gallery's glass facade. But Tuymans deals well (almost flirts) with adversity, and the show made its debut just two months later, comprising work in his characteristically pale, sun-bleached palette and depicting mundane subjects and scenes from his space – including a rare self-portrait – yet with a scrim of enigmatic detachment, making them at once eerily familiar and indescribably foreign.

Tuymans' seemingly simple subject matter – a window, a suit jacket, his leg – shouldn't be taken at face value. He masterfully layers both paint and appropriation – from history, photographs, film, literature – whether visually depicted on the canvas or slid into the sometimes cryptic titles for his large-scale paintings. In his Summer 2012 show at David Zwirner's London space, Tuymans presented a series of paintings (some of which are reproduced in the image section following this interview) that recall early works by Gauguin but via their interpretation in Albert Lewin's 1942 film *THE MOON AND SIXPENCE*, which is loosely based on Gauguin's life.

When we sat down, Tuymans spoke about the evolution of his practice and career, his painting process and struggles as an artist, and subjects ranging from the zoo in his home city of Antwerp to his take on recent Hollywood films and his own penchant for filmmaking.

––––––––––

Q. THE WHITE REVIEW — Can you tell me about this new body of work? I read that you focused on your personal space?

A. LUC TUYMANS — Yeah, well it's not really thematic. In a sense, it's about all the things in my vicinity, and at the same time the fact that they are becoming impenetrable. The show was triggered by Michael Heizer's exhibition here in New York in 2010, which I thought was a beautiful show. He's a land artist, but he had a couple of paintings and a couple of sculptures in this space and it looked very monumental. I had never exhibited in here, though I had shown work in all of the other [Zwirner] spaces. I also wanted to make a show that could be seen in one go – in an un-divided space, something unanimous.

Q. THE WHITE REVIEW — Was the thought that a unanimous space would play to the intimacy of the subject matter?

A. LUC TUYMANS — This show is about the vicinity of things, intimacy, but at the same time it's about the element of austerity.

Q. THE WHITE REVIEW — Where did the title come from?

A. LUC TUYMANS — THE SUMMER IS OVER is derived from a real experience at dinner with a colleague's father. He was suffering from dementia. In a very lucid moment he addressed me and said, 'The summer is really over.' A week later he was dead. This inspired the question, 'Might there be something wrong?' It is important to isolate one portrait, called 'Me', which was the starting point for the show. It comes from a picture my wife took with an iPhone of me in an unguarded moment in our house, sitting in an Eames chair. I like the picture a lot because it's not very flattering, it's quite a harsh representation of life. I haven't made a lot of self-portraits. There are some that were made early on, on paper, that have survived, but I think that this is only the third self-portrait in paint.

Q. THE WHITE REVIEW — I've read that you steer away from these types of intimate or psychological representations of faces, and I would suspect especially your own face?

A. LUC TUYMANS — But this is not psycho-logical; it's just as I would paint any other portrait. The thing is that you see eventually the harshness of it. As in the other paintings, you are not allowed in, to empathise – the glasses [covering the subject's eyes] beam that out. There is also a window, a small window above a door on the facade opposite where I live, which has been cracked for ages: that triggered the juxtaposition of those two things [the painting 'Morning Sun' is shown alongside 'Me']. It is like an outside image, on top of an interior image, but nearly turned inside out. It went on in the painting 'Zoo', which is of [a window at] the back of Antwerp Zoo. That is also a place I see when I drive by cab on the way to my studio. Next to that is a painting of my garden, the city garden, but before it was altered, so it's an older image.

The other painting next to the 'Morning Sun' painting is called 'My Leg', which is an image of my leg taken from the same picture of me in the Eames chair. Then you have 'Jacket', and then 'Wall', which is actually just a projection on the studio wall of an old film still of a film that I made in the eighties in a seaman's hostel in Antwerp that no longer exists. This show is about closure. It deals with the idea of abstraction and figuration. All of these paintings have that capacity, with one exception, which is of course the very distinct and recognisable self-portrait. Even in that, the glasses are predominant because they evade that single reading.

Q. THE WHITE REVIEW — I know you fall outside of the realm of –isms (or perhaps our modern world cannot subscribe to –isms at all) but you have been called a postmodern history painter and a reductive painter and you choose not to ascribe to either of these categories. Are there any one or two words that you can use that do capture your practice, or speak to your oeuvre?

A. LUC TUYMANS — Yes, very simple. There is a Belgian aspect to the work, and also the idea of film documentary, which was a Belgian invention [the Belgian Documentary School, founded by Charles Dekeukeleire and Henri Storck in the 1930s, helped pioneer the genre]. When people talk about Belgium, they talk about two things: Magritte and Ensor, sur-realism and the grotesque, though Magritte was not a surrealist and Ensor was not just grotesque; and then of course they talk about Rubens. But they forget Jan van Eyck, who was the best painter in the Western hemisphere. So this is our trauma, this is what we come from. Belgium is not really romantic. There was never time for it, because the region was involved in so many wars. It means that there is a very real sense of reality, or of the assessment of reality in Belgian art. Reality is perhaps sometimes superseded by a sort of spiritual construction. But it's a spiritual construction born of *visuals*, it is not born out of a flaccid pseudo-intellectual or pseudo-philosophical discourse. So it's very hardcore, the visual culture in my country.

One of my favourite paintings is the 'Arnolfini Marriage', in which you see the mirror and the inscription 'Jan van Eyck was here'. The reflection in a convex mirror opens up the space beyond the canvas. Although van Eyck was part of a religious society, he was nevertheless the very first artist who by heightening the idea of the material and the depiction of the reality of existence itself, opened up the frame to the world. Of course, Velasquez saw that before he made 'Las Meninas'. In a sense, it's very simple, that's where we come from, that's undeniable. It has nothing to do with –isms, it has nothing to do with modernity, or it has a lot to do with modernity, but not in the sense of a linear art historical discourse. It has to do with the genealogical aspect of the visual, which is contained in the physical place from which you come.

Q. THE WHITE REVIEW — When you were in art school what type of paintings were you making?

A. LUC TUYMANS — In the beginning of course I was very naive. I was making very colourful, abstract, gestural sort of paintings.

Q. THE WHITE REVIEW — And then you left to pursue film-making?

A. LUC TUYMANS — Yes, from 1980–85.

Q. THE WHITE REVIEW — Why? Did you continue to paint?

A. LUC TUYMANS — No. During my time at art school it was becoming more and more difficult to paint. The paintings became too existential, too suffocating, too close, physically: it just didn't function, like writer's block. I didn't see any purpose in it anymore. It was by coincidence that a friend who was studying to be an actor approached me. He showed me a Super 8 camera and a lens and I just started to film. I liked it because it was very similar to painting.

Q. THE WHITE REVIEW — In what way?

A. LUC TUYMANS — I was always a bad photographer, because I could never be in the moment, I would always be too late. Paintings are sort of a late medium. Now film, you can actually edit the film in the camera. But filming is about approaching the image like painting is about approaching the image, albeit in a more physical way than filming. And of course you can edit, so these are all things that made it quite familiar. Eventually they took away the Super 8, so I had to go to 16mm and then Super 16 and in the end 35mm, but I wanted to make a movie, which of course financially we couldn't.

Q. THE WHITE REVIEW — A film about what?

A. LUC TUYMANS — Well the film was supposed to be called *LIFE ON EARTH* and it was a semi-documentary about an Indian ship that was stranded in the harbour of a bay. It looked a little bit like *STRANGER THAN PARADISE*. Financially it became a battle, too. When I returned to painting, the image making was informed by this adventure in film, particularly in terms of editing close–ups. And it created more distance for me. Creators need distance.

Q. THE WHITE REVIEW —— Speaking of the close–up, you've spoken about the blurriness in your painting being sharp, precise. I see an element of film in that technique, that style. Can you talk about this precise blurriness in your paintings?

A. LUC TUYMANS —— Well the blurriness, or opaqueness, that sort of skin that comes in front of the canvas, is interesting. At the studio I work onto a piece of canvas nailed to the wall; the canvas isn't stretched. The fascination for me, still to this day, is that once the paintings are finished, they are framed, they change, they become objects. They inherit this additional screen, this additional veil. There's been a lot of talk about this reduction of colour, blurriness. But the show that I did in London [*ALLO!*] was with far less colour than this. These are much more complicated because the tonality is far richer and far more difficult and far more colourful than simple colours like red, blue, yellow. This has also to do with the idea that grey lines are translucent. That's not just a construction, it's a reality within paint and a reality for the mind because it's very difficult to comprehend and it's especially difficult to image, and also the idea of depth. But blurriness in a painterly process would wipe that out, by for instance raking over the material. I don't do that, so all the blurriness is sharp, it is painted; everything is painted.

Q. THE WHITE REVIEW —— There is a thin appearance to the paint that suggests ephem–erality or transience. Is that intentional, some–thing that you're thinking about as you're painting? Or does it lend itself to an evasive quality, something that detaches people from the work?

A. LUC TUYMANS —— Well I'm probably very evasive. I have always been, even to myself [laughs]. Those things are not something that I think about when I'm painting. To conceptualise images takes months; that's the longest period – to find the image, to rework it through maquettes, Polaroids, film, work on the computer. You have to pinpoint this one image that becomes a painting, or which has painterly possibility. When that is realised then the painting is already halfway done. I never work on two paintings at the same time, only one painting. Which I think is also a habitual thing; finishing a painting in a day is not so hard. Once I start painting I don't want to think any more, because at that point it's the hands that take over. I want to keep the intentionality, the intensity, as real as possible. So when I'm painting I'm not thinking about whether it's ephemeral or whether it's this or that. I don't think about those things. I might think about those things when I lay down my brush, and I might say that it looks awful or think that it's stupid, those are doubts, but not during the process of painting. That also means that a lot of paintings are extremely premeditated. There are paintings I actually cherish, like 'Body', which is from 1990, a painting that was really not going anywhere right up until the moment I made two decisive strokes, which really turned the whole show around. There are four, five, six paintings like that, but not a lot.

Q. THE WHITE REVIEW —— Is there any association to subjects such as tragedy, cele–bration, politics, in subject matter that may otherwise seem banal or harmless, such as a window, or a bowl of fruit?

A. LUC TUYMANS —— There are shows that are

quite dramatic, but this is my tenth show with David Zwirner and it goes much further: it becomes monumental, it induces the idea of mortality, as does the title. It's about people painting but it's also about me. So this is a joke aimed at the spectator who wants to have insight into everything about the guy behind the painting, to know what that guy is thinking; of course, the guy is not thinking anything. This is what it is and this is what it will be, and it will not get better, and so this is just what you get.

Q. THE WHITE REVIEW — It will not get better?
A. LUC TUYMANS — No, because it shouldn't. This is the limit of things. Of course, another show will be different, and the show that just finished in Japan is different. The *ALLO!* show was totally different from this. But for this show I wanted to make that ridiculous point, which is on the verge of being pathetic. But it's not at my own expense, it's at the spectator's.

Q. THE WHITE REVIEW — You often talk about false history or false reality. This seems to directly relate to that. I mean, you're suggesting that your work could be entirely false, or misleading.
A. LUC TUYMANS — Of course, but that has always been the rule, throughout my oeuvre. I feel that everyone should be distrustful of what they're looking at. Listening, imagery – it also comes back to my own imagery.

Q. THE WHITE REVIEW — And distrustful of history too?
A. LUC TUYMANS — Everything.

Q. THE WHITE REVIEW — Have you distrusted your own personal history as well as Western history?
A. LUC TUYMANS — Yes, because I think

histories are inconsequential and certainly incomplete. Memory is inadequate, and history tends to be falsified.

Q. THE WHITE REVIEW — Does that mean a good painting can be a painting that cannot be remembered?
A. LUC TUYMANS — Yes.

Q. THE WHITE REVIEW — You've spoken a bit about working from photographic sources, and you talk about the process and about re-photographing them.
A. LUC TUYMANS — Well, the original images are just made on an iPhone. Apart from that, they are sought-out images, re-created, re-made, re-used, and then made political and painterly.

Q. THE WHITE REVIEW — Is it often the composition of the image that you're looking at? Is it the subject matter?
A. LUC TUYMANS — More often than not it's the subject matter first, and then the composition.

Q. THE WHITE REVIEW — And then the context? Where you are physically when you see something; does that ever play a part?
A. LUC TUYMANS — It may or may not do, it depends. The image of the zoo came across because of the environment more than anything else. So the idea was already formulated there and then, very much skewed, so you could not enter this windowpane, which is translucent normally, but is here dusty.

Q. THE WHITE REVIEW — I read an interview with you in which you spoke effusively about the film *THERE WILL BE BLOOD*, and particularly about the opening in which there's no dialogue for fifteen minutes. It makes me think about the quality of your work: there's an element to the work that's so subtle you can almost miss it, yet there's this tension between that subtlety and a very aggressive quality, which also occurs throughout the film.

A. LUC TUYMANS — Yes, THERE WILL BE BLOOD was quite exceptional. That year there were three movies in the mainstream that were quite exceptional: CONTROL by Anton Corbijn, which was a beautiful first film. Then there was NO COUNTRY FOR OLD MEN, and the cherry on the cake was THERE WILL BE BLOOD and the first fifteen minutes of those epic landscapes, of a person just doing something, with virtually no sound either. Of course it's a story about greed and oil – but the film largely transgresses its story through the perfect performance of Daniel Day–Lewis and the fact that it's basically about anger–management. Each of those three films are about desperation or anger, and how it can get totally out of control, and in that sense, in a very minimalistic way, those three films achieved something that the artworld had not yet understood, which I thought was quite amazing. Those three films are really about the human condition: there was this overt tension between those underlying structures and the moving images. That is a risk in mainstream cinema, and it was quite something to see.

Q. THE WHITE REVIEW — You are renowned for finishing paintings very quickly. Do you experience that urgency as limiting, or liberating?

A. LUC TUYMANS — It's just that I have a limited attention span, and also I don't have a lot of patience. I really have to see something before I leave, before I close the door of my studio.

Q. THE WHITE REVIEW — And what percentage of paintings you start do you finish in one day?

A. LUC TUYMANS — All of them.

Q. THE WHITE REVIEW — What happens if you are not happy with a painting?

A. LUC TUYMANS — Nowadays I have the luxury of being able to throw it away but in the early days I would paint over it.

Q. THE WHITE REVIEW — And you never return to a painting?

A. LUC TUYMANS — No I do, in the sense that there are little, little details that I adjust.

Q. THE WHITE REVIEW — What do you feel when you look at a blank canvas?

A. LUC TUYMANS — Horror.

Q. THE WHITE REVIEW — And when you don't like a painting, how does that feel?

A. LUC TUYMANS — Horrible. [Laughs]

Q. THE WHITE REVIEW — Do you know whether a painting is successful as soon as it is finished?

A. LUC TUYMANS — It takes a while. It takes a while and it doesn't, it's essentially the first hour, or a couple of hours after the painting, and of course I know very well what I'm doing when I start a painting. Still, it is so intensified as a moment and so loaded that, for the first few hours, I don't know what the fuck I'm doing, but after that I do. So once the visibility of the image falls together, that's the point when either it succeeds, or I can at least see the direction it is going in, and then the joy of painting kicks in. But that's not the case in the beginning. I think that's the same in every artistic process; the beginning is the worst.

Q. THE WHITE REVIEW — What is your painting environment like, your studio?

A. LUC TUYMANS — The studio that I've worked the most in is a very small apartment where I used to live and work at the same time, which was of course horrible. Since 2006 I have had a big studio.

Q. THE WHITE REVIEW —— Is it somewhat masochistic that you used to live in the same studio as you worked in?

A. LUC TUYMANS —— No, it was sheer economic necessity. But I held onto that one space, even when I moved in with my girlfriend. I was really hooked on having it look like Francis Bacon's studio [the notoriously chaotic South Kensington work space transplanted upon the artist's death to Dublin City Gallery The Hugh Lane], whereas now my studio looks like a professional studio with daylight coming from above. I was very afraid when moving into the new studio that that would be a problem, but it wasn't.

Q. THE WHITE REVIEW —— A problem in what way?

A. LUC TUYMANS —— Just to work there, because I lost my...

Q. THE WHITE REVIEW —— Comfort?

A. LUC TUYMANS —— No, not my comfort, just an environment that I had built up. But it wasn't the case, it was actually better.

Q. THE WHITE REVIEW —— How does Antwerp, the city in which you live, play a part in your painting practice, in terms of actual physical space?

A. LUC TUYMANS —— The good thing about Antwerp is that everything is quite close and accessible. There's something about the light, too. If I were to move to Los Angeles or to Spain I would make quite different paintings, because of the different light, so in that sense the place influences the imagery. When the retrospective show of my work moved from the United States to Brussels and was shown

in the Palais des Beaux-Arts, the four curators mentioned in their introductions that it was a blast to see the paintings in the light that they were painted in. It does make a big difference.

Q. THE WHITE REVIEW —— Do you think painting has evolved, or is painting always about a moment in a particular space, and not necessarily a real space or time?

A. LUC TUYMANS —— Painting is about painted time, not about real time. That's a major illusion within perception itself. A painting is created out of elements that are known, that we are inept to talk about, or are visual, or are very physical, and the physicality of the practice itself and its result, which is why the after-image of the practice is so detailed and so difficult to retrace, not only for the spectator, but maybe even for the person who made the painting, although I mostly still know where I started and where I ended. But it is a very complex situation.

Q. THE WHITE REVIEW —— Have you considered revisiting film?

A. LUC TUYMANS —— Maybe, I don't know. There is still this sort of an underbelly feeling that one day I should do something...

Q. THE WHITE REVIEW —— Is there any question that I haven't asked, or that no journalist has ever asked, that you think they should?

A. LUC TUYMANS —— No.

MARINA CASHDAN, JANUARY 2013

Allo!

TOPSOIL

BY

JESSE LONCRAINE

THE EVENING HAD SPRING IN IT. Faintly sweet and peppery. To disturb a small tree sent birds chattering skyward. Weeks before there had been no birds anywhere. Hector watched them scatter like shrapnel. Whatever colour they were, the birds looked black against the purple sky. He drove a pitchfork into the marked patch of ground with the heel of his boot. Levered the teeth backwards and forwards, grinding his way into the thawing earth.

A youngish woman watched him from the driver's seat of a 4x4 parked at the edge of the field. The vehicle was the only one in sight. They were far from the main road.

Hector dropped to his knees and turned a grabbing of topsoil in his hand. He said a prayer and crossed himself – forehead to chest, right shoulder to left.

The woman in the car honked the horn and he felt the sound in the earth.

'Damn you, Martha,' he said, 'I'm coming.'

He rose and made his way back through the field to the car where Martha was tapping a beat on the steering wheel. She ran her fingers through cropped hair, and turned the key in the ignition.

'Well?' she asked over the sound of the engine.

'We start tomorrow.'

'I knew it. What did I tell you? Spring.'

'Yes.'

'About time.'

'Come on,' said Hector, 'let's go.'

¶ Hector arrived home and sat with his wife, Jelena, while she cooked their dinner. She uncapped a bottle of Tuborg and poured it into a glass which she placed in front of him on the dining table. He thanked her and gulped down the cold beer.

'I was working in the garden today while you were gone. The ground has finally softened.'

'You're right, it has.'

'Will you start digging soon then?'

'Tomorrow.'

'Tomorrow? As soon as that?'

Jelena placed a bowl of vegetable soup in front of her husband and a basket of sliced white bread in the centre of the table. Hector took a piece of the bread and dipped it into the steaming bowl of soup. He watched intently as the liquid crept up the length of the bread. Jelena brought her own bowl to the table and sat down opposite him.

'Tell me what you're thinking.'

Hector raised his eyes to meet his wife's. He smiled and popped the soggy bread

F

into his mouth and sucked out the broth. The bread formed a sweet dumpling in the shape of the roof of his mouth.

'I'm thinking we deserve a holiday.'

'*Ho-li-day*. The word sounds vaguely familiar.'

'Once I finish my work, I promise.'

'You know I'm only teasing.'

Hector took a sip of the soup and pushed his bowl to one side. Jelena watched him. She frowned at the unfinished meal.

'I'm sorry. It's delicious. I'm just not hungry tonight.'

'You should eat.'

Hector shrugged. He waited for his wife to finish her soup before lighting a cigarette. Jelena took her own packet of cigarettes from a pocket in her apron and lit up, too. They breathed smoke out the side of their mouths and Jelena stroked her husband's leg beneath the table. She knew what he was thinking.

After smoking, Jelena stood and cleared their plates. She poured Hector's soup back into the pot and left the bowls in the sink to wash up later.

'How about something sweet? Will you eat some chocolate?'

'Thank you, darling. Nothing. I'll eat in the morning. I'll have a stomach for it then.'

He got up from the table and stooped to kiss Jelena on the forehead. She had married a giant, almost seven feet tall. Many women were scared by Hector's height, but Jelena found it attractive. When they slept, she pulled one of his heavy limbs on top of her and passed the night almost crushed under its weight. That was how she liked to sleep, with her husband's immense body burying her. But Hector's body was consuming itself of late. He ate less and less, and only then when she badgered him. His hands and feet and head were starting to look unbalanced, comical, as the muscle slipped away from the bones. Jelena said nothing about his drinking because she knew the beer gave him much-needed calories. She added extra cream and butter to their meals wherever she could, but it only seemed to make her grow fatter.

¶ In the living room, they sat together on the couch with Jelena's legs resting on her husband's lap. Hector read over his notes while Jelena watched an old cartoon on the television with the sound muted.

'Tomorrow, maybe I'll come with you.'

Hector tipped his glasses and looked at his wife.

'Come with me where?'

'On the dig.'

He rested his notes on her legs and laid his hand on her hip.

'What's brought this on?'

'I've been having nightmares. My imagination's been running wild lately. Today, in the garden, I thought that maybe coming with you would help soothe my mind.'

'Nightmares? About what?'

'About what's beneath us, in the ground.'

'We know what's there. It's simply a matter of finding it.'

Jelena turned back to the television. She felt his eyes on the side of her face. A cartoon mouse peered out of a hole in the wall, surveying the room for danger. The shadow of a cat tiptoed across the wall and the mouse retreated back inside his hole.

'So, will you let me come with you?'

'I don't think it's a good idea.'

'Maybe not. But still, I'd like to come this once.'

'Very well. Martha is collecting me at five.'

'I'll be ready.'

Strewn about the coffee table were Jelena's books of sheet music. Hector moved a pile carefully to one side and put his feet up.

'How's your composition going?' Hector asked.

'I haven't played once in four days. I can't seem to concentrate. Perhaps it's the changing of seasons. I don't know. I remember even when I was a child I found the melting snow extremely depressing. Other children were excited because it meant summer was on its way, but I was always sad when winter ended.'

'My melancholy crocus,' he said, and lifted her legs off his lap and folded his glasses into his shirt pocket. 'I'm going to bed. Are you coming?'

'I'll be up soon. I just want to clear up a little.'

Jelena rose from the sofa and went to the kitchen to wash the dishes and cover the soup. Standing at the sink, she looked out into the garden, still bare from the long winter. There was a moon and hardly any stars. If she squinted, she could just make out the mounds of disturbed soil where she had dug the holes that morning. Perhaps she'd known she would find nothing, but it helped to know that she was looking too, that she was helping Hector with his work.

❡ A cold mud swallowed her bare feet as she trudged through the open field. It had rained and her dress grew heavy at the back where it trailed along the ground, collecting the grey mud. She was glad to be there, in spite of the biting air. Towards the middle of the field, she could see Hector and his team, busy working, digging in the white halogen glare of their spotlights, their shovels seeming like mechanical arms, rhythmically snatching at the earth and depositing it in mounds at their feet. A generator hummed nearby. She admired the beauty of their efficient labouring, like some socialist mural of the country at work.

Suddenly she was naked and cold. Her clothes lay discarded behind her in the muddy field. The wind blew her hair into her mouth and eyes. It stung her nipples.

She knelt down and plastered her breasts in a layer of mud then spread her knees and took another handful and ran the mud between her legs, covering herself. The wetted soil clung to her pubic hair, forming into thick, stalactitic clumps. A plane roared overhead and when she looked up she could just make out her name on the undercarriage in iridescent lettering. She watched as it dwindled to a speck in the sky, until all that was left was a slowly evaporating vapour trail.

Lifting her legs grew harder as she walked. Each step caked her feet in new layers of mud, making her legs feel unnaturally heavy. Soon the mud rose around her ankles and her feet sank further into the ground. She gripped her right leg at the knee and pulled her foot free, planting it a step in front. She did the same with her left leg and proceeded like that for a few metres – prizing one leg free and then the other. Finally the effort was too much and she gave in and just stood there, planted in the ground up to her calves, feeling herself not so slowly sinking. Within minutes her knees had disappeared, and soon the mud held her upper thighs like tight-fitting stockings. She splayed her buttocks with her hands and let the mud slip between them. Her body was suddenly hot and feverish. As she sunk below her navel, her breath quickened. She raised her arms and allowed her stomach and chest to sink into the clinging earth.

❡ Jelena's eyes shot open and the pain of Hector inside her ripped through her body as if she had been staked alive. She writhed beneath his weight and screamed at him:

'Get off me. Get off me.'

Hector pulled himself out of her and rolled away, a look of confusion and fear on his face.

'What's wrong? What did I do?'

'What were you *doing* to me?'

'What was I doing?'

'You were, you were in my–'

'It wasn't me. You put it there.'

'I put it there? Are you fucking crazy, Hector?'

'Jesus, Jelena, calm down. Were you asleep?'

'Of course I was asleep. What did you do to me?'

'I didn't do anything. You rolled over and rubbed yourself against me until I was awake and then you took me with your hand and put me inside you, in there.'

She scanned her husband's face in the half-light and then got out of bed and stormed to the bathroom. She locked the door. Hector called after her:

'Jelena, come back. Are you okay?'

He could hear her crying through the door as he wrestled with the handle.

'Let me in.'

'Go away.'

'Please, Jelena. Let me in. Are you hurt?'

'No. Leave me alone.'

Hector retreated to the bed and switched on a lamp. The clock showed 3.50 a.m., just over an hour until Martha came to collect him. He pulled back the bed covers. There were spots of blood on the sheets.

'Jelena,' he called, 'are you okay?'

'I'm fine. Leave. Me. Alone.'

He pulled on some underwear and went downstairs. In the kitchen he went over in his mind what had happened – just as he had told her. He hadn't done anything wrong. He hadn't initiated anything. Still, the thought of his wife upstairs alone, crying, bleeding, made him nauseous. He lit a cigarette to calm his nerves.

Jelena sat on the toilet bent forward with her arms wrapped around her stomach. She tore some sheets of paper from the roll and used them to touch herself gently where it stung. She winced from the pain, took in short, sharp breaths. When she looked at the paper it was red. The pain was interior too, dull and throbbing. She sat on the toilet for ten minutes willing herself not to cry. Eventually she stood and turned on the shower and waited for the water to run as hot as it would go. The almost scolding heat of the water on her neck and back. Once the shock had mostly subsided, Jelena felt her nerves calming. Slowly, her thoughts shifted to Hector downstairs, and to his empty stomach. She finished showering, dried off, and placed a sanitary towel in the seat of her knickers. Back in their bedroom she pulled on some jeans and a loose-fitting shirt and fixed her hair in the mirror – a simple bun on top of her head. Before going downstairs she made the bed.

'Will you eat some eggs?' she asked.

'There's no need. I can make something.'

'Will you eat eggs, or won't you?'

'Jelena, I'm sorry.'

'Forget about it.'

'Are you okay?'

'I'm fine.'

'You promise?'

'Martha will be here soon. Go get dressed. I'll make us some breakfast.'

¶ It was about an hour's drive to the site. They passed early commuters en route to the factories outside of town with their heads bowed low and hooded against the cold. Some of the men held out their thumbs in hope of a lift. They gave the impression of being devout men on some pilgrimage to who knew where.

Jelena was drifting off to sleep when Martha swerved to avoid a drunk who lurched into the road, suddenly and with intent. She leant out the window and shouted a string of foreign curses. Jelena turned in her seat and watched the drunk man as he chicken-danced behind them in the dark.

'So Jelena, how do you like it, living here?' asked Martha.

'I like it fine. It's a good place to write.'

'Why's that?'

'There are very few distractions.'

'It's boring as hell, in other words.'

Jelena smiled. It was not exactly what she meant.

'Personally, I can't wait to get out of here. The food stinks and the men are all miserable drunks, aren't they, Hector?'

He nodded that they were.

From the backseat, Jelena noticed the bald patch on her husband's head, a new part of him unknown to his former lovers. She reached forward and squeezed his shoulder as Martha signalled right and slowed down. They turned off the tarmac and onto an unpaved road, lined on either side by naked trees – the forest the last remaining sanctuary of winter. After a mile they arrived at a simple wooden gate manned by two soldiers. Martha brought the vehicle to a crawl and flashed an ID card. The soldiers greeted them with frosty breaths and waved on the 4x4. Jelena caught Hector's eye in the rear-view mirror – his thick eyebrows pinched together in a slight frown. She could tell that the soldiers made him uneasy. They drove on. The road climbing steadily.

'We're nearly there,' said Hector.

'It's chilling to think they came along this road,' said Jelena. Hector nodded, but as Jelena spoke the words she knew they sounded forced, out of place. She wished she'd said nothing.

They rounded a bend and the trees gave way to a large open field. It was not as she'd imagined. There were several other cars with their engines running, and Hector's men trekked back and forth with heavy equipment, shouting to each other, laughing. Rusted farm tools and old water containers lay strewn about in ugly heaps. A faint daylight was beginning to show the contours of the land. The field was mounded and irregular, the soil untilled for years.

'Don't get in the way,' said Hector, jumping out of the car before it had even stopped.

'Ignore him,' said Martha, turning back to Jelena, 'he gets like this out here.'

Jelena got out of the car and watched Hector giving orders, impressed by the way her husband moved around, directing his team without hesitation. Looking at him radiating energy in that bleak place, Jelena found him intensely attractive. She imagined herself lying down with him there, in the field, beneath him, between him

F

and the ground.

Hector's men pulled white jumpsuits over their clothes and measured out a twelve by twelve square beside a crooked tree in the northwest corner of the field. They marked the four corners with wooden stakes and joined them together with lengths of string, setting the perimeter in place. Then they began to dig, methodically, a foot deep across the entire square, depositing the earth on blue tarpaulin sheets. A second team sifted through the excavated mounds with hand trowels, creating smaller subdivided piles of rocks and wood and filtered soil. Martha circled the scene with a digital camera, taking photos and making notes in a small leather-bound book. Hector checked his watch and the rising sun.

Jelena went and stood beside her husband. She offered him a cigarette.

'No, thank you.'

'Do you mind if I have one?'

'No, go ahead.'

'Why do you think they chose this place?'

'Most likely because of the tree. This corner of the field wouldn't have been farmed. That makes it much less likely to be discovered.'

'But there's a whole forest. Why would they come out here, in the open?'

'The root systems are too dense in the forest. It's harder to dig.'

The men had stopped. Hector moved away from his wife and conferred with a man in a white paisley bandana. She watched them take handfuls of soil and feel its texture between their fingers as they talked. Hector made some motion towards the square and the man in the bandana nodded. Hector patted him on the shoulder and soon the men were digging again. Another foot of soil was removed, the process of sifting repeated. A measuring stick was driven into the ground as they dug further down. They worked in near silence, only a young woman listening to music and humming a barely audible melody as she troweled the mounded earth.

'What were you talking about, just then, with—'

'Alberto. I was asking his opinion on the subsoil. He can tell from the density if it's been dug up before.'

'What did he say?'

'He said it has.'

'That's a good thing?'

'It means we're in the right place, yes.'

As absentmindedly as if they were in bed, Jelena reached for her husband's hand. He turned to her:

'What is it?'

'I'm sorry. Nothing. I wasn't thinking.'

Jelena drew her hand away. She guessed that he was angry with her for coming, but she didn't care. She needed to be there. Her presence was something Hector would simply have to abide.

The first rays of sun warmed the back of Jelena's neck, and her body and the tree cast a shadow over the deepening pit. Two of the men drew sunglasses from their breast pockets, which seemed strange in the soft morning light and the shadows. The woman with the headphones raised her hand and Martha jogged two sides of the square and knelt down beside her. She quickly signalled for Hector to join them. The others had stopped digging and were watching Martha.

'A baby's shoe?' said Martha, placing the scrap of leather in Hector's palm.

'You're sure it's a shoe?' he asked.

'That's what it looks like.'

Hector's jaw stiffened and his eyes narrowed to a concentrated stare.

'May I see it?' asked Jelena.

Hector handed her the earth-filled shoe, little bigger than a packet of cigarettes. Jelena turned it over in her hand, traced her fingers along the sole, and over the brittle tongue. Time and the elements had turned the leather hard.

'She's right.'

'Please, everyone' said Hector, 'keep digging. Martha, bag this.'

Hector returned to his spot beneath the tree, crouched on his knees and scratched his beard. He barely seemed to notice Jelena, still at his side.

'Hector, are there children here?'

'Must you keep asking so many questions? Didn't I tell you not to get in the way?'

'I'm sorry. It's just, I thought you said it was only men.'

'The shoe, if that's even what it is, could be from anywhere. It was in topsoil. Topsoil changes over time. It lies. Animals come from the forest and dig around looking for food. The rains drag soil from further uphill. It was probably left here by some family picnicking in the shade. You can't trust what you find until you get further down.'

Beads of sweat glistened on Alberto's tanned forehead. Every few minutes he rested his shovel against the side of the pit and wiped his brow with a corner of cloth from his breast pocket. Jelena had met him once before, at a dinner for Hector's team back in the autumn. Alberto had praised her cooking. She smiled at him now, and he nodded. His overalls were unzipped and tied at the waist. He wore a T-shirt on which a dark grey lake of perspiration was spreading outwards from the centre of his back. When his men were chest-deep, Alberto called for the buckets to be lowered into the pit to carry the soil up to ground level. He looked up at Hector and shrugged. Still nothing.

Martha wandered over and stood beside Hector and sighed.

'We're at four feet, Hec.'

'Never mind that. Alberto said—'

'I know what Alberto said. I'm just saying we should be prepared for the possibility that this isn't what we were expecting.'

It seemed to Jelena like sound advice, but Hector waved it away with a hand in front of his face, swiping at an imaginary fly.

'This is the place.'

'How can you be sure?' Jelena asked, but Hector only stared into the pit in silence. The morning drew on without discovery.

¶ At the first glimpse of bone, Alberto replaced the shovels with more precise tools and Hector clambered down into the grave and dusted the earth from an adult male skull. He inspected it quietly, peering into the cavities and turning it carefully in his hands. The others watched as he re-enacted the execution – placing a finger on the base of Alberto's skull – demonstrating how the bullet entered through a small hole in the back of the cranium, and exploded out the front, just above the eyes, leaving a three-inch exit wound with its sharp, fragmented edges.

The skull was passed around in a sort of ritual. Each member of the team held it for a moment, some raised it slightly into the sun like the passing of a sporting trophy. When the skull reached Martha, she placed it on a numbered tray and photographed it from several angles. The men returned to the pit where the bones appeared now like eagerly sprouting bulbs woken by the changing season. They came up from the ground one after another for the next four hours: femur, clavicle, tibia, ribs, humerus. Efforts were made to keep the skeletons intact, but the bodies had fallen into the pit one on top of another, and with the decaying of the flesh the bones had mingled, without their soft exteriors to define them, so that each corpse was indiscernible from the next: scapula, sternum, sacrum – a continuous chain of human remains and two gold molars glinting from jaws smiling at the midday sun.

The final skull count was seventeen when Alberto hit rock and the grave was declared exhumed. All the victims were grown males. Several bullet casings were recovered among the bodies. No clothes were found – the men had been buried naked. No engraved wedding rings, no stopped watches, no dog tags, only a single glass eye, with an iris that polished sky-blue. Boxes were brought from the trucks at the edge of the field and the bones carefully labelled.

Hector was the last to emerge from the grave. Jelena stood at ground level and looked down at her husband, sitting with his back against the wall of the pit. His eyes were closed and she could see that he was talking to himself or perhaps saying a prayer.

'Hector.'

He opened his eyes and looked up at Jelena, silhouetted against the afternoon sky.

'I'm coming down.'

'Don't bother. There's nothing to see. I'm coming up now anyway. It's cold and damp down here.'

Hector climbed out of the pit using a rope ladder tied to the trunk of the tree. He kissed his wife on the forehead, gathered his things from a pile at the edge of the pit and headed towards the cars.

'Hector, wait.'

'What is it?'

'Do you think they were brought here naked?'

'It's unlikely. They came here alive, were stripped, and made to stand at the edge of the pit, where you're standing now. All the wounds are the same. One by one, they were killed with a single bullet to the back of the head, and they fell directly into the pit.'

'What do you think in that moment when you're standing in the cold, naked, waiting to be executed?'

'Most people cover their private parts. They feel humiliated, even though they know they're about to die.'

'...'

'Let's go. Martha's waiting.'

Hector and Jelena crossed the field in silence. Halfway back to the cars, Jelena stopped and turned around.

'What is it?' Hector asked.

'Nothing, go on. There's something I want to see. Wait for me in the car. I won't be long.'

Before Hector could object, Jelena set off running back across the field. Her bun slipped out as she ran and her hair danced red on her shoulders. At the tree, she reached out her hand and bent forward, catching her breath a moment. She looked back at him briefly and then Hector watched as she climbed down the rope ladder and disappeared from sight. He turned to see if his team was watching, but they were busy loading the equipment into the vehicles and hadn't noticed. Only Martha was looking, and he wasn't concerned if she saw Jelena's strange behaviour. He often confided to Martha about the problems in his marriage. Hector wondered if he should go and fetch his wife, but returning to the grave might draw the attention of his crew. He remained where he was, waiting for her to reappear. Hector grew more restless with each passing minute. A flock of geese soared overhead.

Three minutes passed. His restlessness changed to concern when it occurred to him that in her haste Jelena might have fallen from the rope ladder and broken her ankle, or worse. Martha had lost interest and put her seat back so that all he could see was her hand draped casually out the driver's side window, a cigarette between her mannish fingers.

He checked his watch, as if that might hurry Jelena along. The strange night, their somnambulistic sexual encounter, which had drifted from his thoughts over the course of the day, returned to him. His pulse quickened and he had a sudden feeling that Jelena wanted him to follow her – that she was waiting for him at the bottom of the pit. The men were still busy. He pictured Jelena sprawled naked in the dirt. Had she not undone her hair with a flick of her wrist as she ran? He took a stride towards the tree. Another. His feet felt heavy, as if they were reluctant to follow. He prized each foot from the ground. A determination to love his wife, to fuck her, welled up like something fermenting in his gut. And then Jelena's head appeared above ground. She hoisted herself out of the pit and retied the thick mane of hair above her head. Hector stopped. He watched her come towards him. When she reached him, she kept walking.

'I told you to wait in the car,' she said.

'What were you doing?'

'I just wanted to see what it was like down there.'

On the drive home Jelena lay across the back seats of the 4x4 and slept. She heard Martha and Hector talking in the front, but nothing of what they said, only the sound of their voices and the rise and fall of the road as they drove through the hills.

¶ Anna could see them walking around up there, above her – no way that they could see or hear her buried so deep underground. She opened her mouth to call out to them but bits of earth fell onto her tongue and into the back of her throat and choked her. An earthworm worked its way into her nose and she could feel it, like thick snot, curl itself around her uvula as she gagged. She watched them passing over her with their digging tools and felt the vibrations in the earth as they broke ground near to where she was buried. Not near enough and they would miss her and she would be left there to rot.

It began to rain and she could feel the rain seeping down through the soil and wetting her skin, and soon the weeds were pushing their way out of her pores and out of the ground and uncurling into small flowers that the men trampled with their work boots. She cried out for them to stop treading on her, but they still couldn't hear.

Bits of her were bone – her feet and ribs and skull, and bits were flesh – her breasts and hips and buttocks. An assembly of body parts decaying, each in their own time. Her eyelids opening and closing. Her heart still beating strongly inside her muddied ribcage. The men were above her now, coming directly down with the bladed edges of their shovels, slicing the earth apart like meatloaf, severing tough tree roots with single strikes.

How will they know to stop when they reach me, she wondered.

They did not. Hector struck first. His shovel cleaved off her right hand at the wrist and she felt the metal against her bone and her fingers curling around a rock in their last ditched effort to reach for something and hold it. Hector shovelled out her dismembered hand and showed it to the other men. One of the men used her hand to feel and prod the groin of another and everyone laughed.

¶ Hector woke up drenched in sweat and alone in the bed. Light showed through the crack beneath the bathroom door. He pulled his sodden T-shirt over his head, and slipped out of his shorts, and sat there naked with his feet on the floor, panting in the dark. He recalled the early days of their love affair, long before Jelena, when he lived in New York and she had just published her book. The launch in Midtown where his friend introduced them:

'Anna, meet Hector. A fellow exile.'

She shook his hand. 'It's a pleasure to meet you, Hector.'

'Likewise.'

'Hector digs up bones,' said his friend.

'A palaeontologist?'

'Forensics', Hector corrected. 'What is your book about?' he asked.

'It's a history. Please, help yourself to a copy. They're over there on that table.'

They got drunk at the event and he invited her back to his apartment. They seemed to fuck forever. She felt so tiny next to him, like a stuffed animal, or a doll, in his bed.

'I came inside you,' he said.

'It's okay,' she said, 'I'm on the pill.'

He pulled her close to him and they fell asleep entwined, and when he woke in the morning she was gone, but she had left her phone number on a pad by the side of his bed. A week later, he called her and she came over and they repeated the sex. By the third or fourth week they had decided to move back home, against the advice of their friends. The night before she disappeared she asked him if he thought they would both survive the war.

'Of course,' he said.

'How can you be so sure?' she asked.

Hector got out of bed, pulled on a fresh pair of shorts and went downstairs. The house was silent. He looked at the clock on the wall above the refrigerator. An hour until Martha picked him up. He opened the fridge and looked for something to eat, but he wasn't hungry so he sat at the kitchen table and smoked a cigarette. He heard the padding of Jelena's feet on the stairs and then he felt her hands on his shoulders, rubbing them.

'Let me make you something to eat,' she said.

F

'You're too good to me,' said Hector.

'Yes,' she said, 'you're probably right,' and patted the bald spot on the top of his head.

He ate the eggs she placed in front of him dutifully, though they tasted mainly of butter and were too rich for him. When Martha pulled into their driveway and beeped her horn, Hector was still at the table in his underwear.

'Please tell her I'll be out in a minute,' he said as he raised himself up off the chair and left the room to get ready.

THE PRESENT HOUR

BY

YVES BONNEFOY

(*tr.* BEVERLEY BIE BRAHIC)

LE NOM PERDU

I

Un vieil home, à même le sol
Devant l'hôtel, à deux pas de la plage.
Il dit qu'il va mourir,
On se penche sur lui, il se détourne.

Il dit encore
Qu'il voudrait que tout vaque à son ordinaire
Autour de lui, dans ce lieu de hasard,
Que les gens entrent et sortent,

Que les servantes chantent en dressant les tables,
Qu'elles rient avec les clients.
Et pourtant, à l'adolescent qui s'agenouille :

« Ah, prend ce livre, dit-il,
Un nom est là.
Dis-moi ce nom que je cherche. »

II

Ce livre,
Des pages déchirées qu'il tient serrées.
Deux ombres sous des vitres tachées de boue.
Peut-être est-ce le reste d'un annuaire.

Il desserre ses doigts. Des feuilles tombent.
« Rassemble-les, implore-t-il, le nom est là,
Hélas, parmi tout ces autres. » Il dit encore,
Oui, qu'il est là, qu'il l'a su.

P

THE MISSING NAME

I

An old man, lying on the ground
In front of the hotel, steps from the beach.
He says he's going to die;
People approach, he turns away.

He says again
That everything should go on as usual
Around him here, in this chance place:
Let the guests come and go,

Waitresses sing as they set the tables
And laugh with the guests.
Still, to the adolescent who kneels down:

'Ah,' he says, 'take this book,
There's a name in it.
Tell me this name that I seek.'

II

This book,
A sheaf of torn pages he clutches.
Two shadows, under mud-splashed glass.
Maybe what's left of a directory.

He loosens his fingers. Leaves fall.
'Gather them up,' he pleads, 'the name is there,
Alas, with all the others.' He repeats,
Yes, that it's in there, that he knew it.

Dans d'autres mondes
Des vagues drossent le ciel contre la terre.
Deux enfants s'éloignent sans fin sur une plage.

Il a fermé ses yeux, il tend
Ce qui lui reste du livre. « Dis-moi, dit-il,
Le nom qui consume le livre. »

III

Un nom?
Quelque chose de rond et de lumineux,
Immobile
Comme celui de la servante de Proust.

Ah, oui! À bout portant faire feu!
Le blesser à l'épaule, lui qui se dresse!
Qu'il tressaille, retombe
Apaisé dans la vie qui sera sans fin!

Je vois ces deux
Qui se parlent. L'un aide l'autre
À se mettre debout. Puis ils s'éloignent.

Le fils soutient le père, ils disparaissent
Au bout du quai, près du tas de charbon.
Leur départ, c'est étrange comme la nuit.

In other worlds
Waves drive the sky against the earth.
Two children walk endlessly down a beach.

He has closed his eyes; he holds out
What's left of the book. 'Tell me,' he says,
'The name that consumes the book.'

III

A name?
Something round and luminous,
Immobile
Like that of Proust's housekeeper.

Yes, yes! Point blank, fire!
Wound him in the shoulder, he's getting up!
Let him twitch, fall back
At peace in the life that will be without end!

I see those two
Talking together. One helps the other
To his feet. They walk off.

The son supports the father, they disappear
Where the quay ends, near the pile of coal.
Their departure – it's strange like the night.

P

LA RÉVOLUTION LA NUIT

« Père, ne vois-tu pas que je brûle ? » Mais lui,
Non, il laisse les portes battre, le feu prend
De couloir en couloir dans son destin,
Il n'y a plus de portes, rien que des flammes.

Et c'est vrai : à quoi bon désirer
Mais sans pouvoir ? Avoir voulu parler
Mais sans phrases pour dire ? Avoir regret
Mais seul, et sans qu'un autre ait pu comprendre ?

L'oubli a recouvert le peu qu'il fut,
Il me parut qu'il disait non à l'espérance,
Ne voulant que le feu pour le bois mort.

Nous allions par des rues, parfois, le soir.
Rouge en était le bout sur l'avenue,
Mais nous ne savions rien, nous ne parlions pas.

THE REVOLUTION THE NIGHT

'Father, don't you see I'm burning?' But he,
No, he lets doors bang; the fire ignites
Hallway after hallway of his destiny,
No more doors now nothing but flames.

And it's true: what use to want so much
But without being able? Having longed to speak,
But without the words to say? Feel regret
But alone: nobody could understand.

Oblivion has covered what little he was;
To me it seemed that he said no to hope,
Wanting only the fire for the dead wood.

Some evenings we'd go walking in the streets.
Down at the end the avenue was red.
But we knew nothing, we didn't speak.

IL S'ÉLOIGNE

Dans ce lavis, ébauche d'un paysage,
On le vit s'éloigner. Hésitant d'abord,
Puis prenant ce chemin après quoi cet autre
Et d'autres, d'autres encore, jusqu'à sa nuit.

Ceux qui l'aimaient
N'aperçurent bientôt qu'un reste clair
De sa couleur, un rouge, sous ce ciel
Qui ourle d'inconnu notre rivage.

Grands arbres de là–bas, serrés, impénétrables,
Il avance, immobile, nous ne savons
S'il veut s'aventurer dans leur autre monde.

Ou comme le soleil qui achève sa tâche
S'il pose ses pinceaux, et va s'étendre
En paix, sur la dalle de pierre du ciel du soir.

HE GOES OFF

In this wash, a sketch for a landscape,
They watched him depart. Uncertain at first,
Then taking this road, then that
And others, still others, into his night.

Those who loved him
Soon saw only a bright remains
Of colour, his red, under this sky
Which hems with the unknown our shores.

Tall trees of over there, thick, impenetrable,
He walks on, immobile, we don't know
Whether he wants to venture into their other world.

Or if, like the sun whose work is done,
He drops his brushes, and goes to stretch out
In peace, on the stone slab of the evening sky.

ON THE EXAGGERATED REPORTS OF THE DECLINE OF BRITISH FICTION

BY

JENNIFER HODGSON
& PATRICIA WAUGH

'THE SPECIAL FATE OF THE NOVEL,' FRANK KERMODE has written, 'is always to be dying.' In Britain, the terminal state seems indigenous to the culture. Beating our chests about the lassitude of novel writing appears to be a critical tradition in its own right. Our last literary season has long passed, it's generally agreed. What-ever happened to the British novel? Well, according to folklore it succumbed to the inclement weather of later consumer culture, or the New Philistinism, or the dumbing down of a compromised welfare consensus, or the paralysing legacies of modernism or a post-imperial loss of status. These days, we might lay the blame for the troubled fate of the British novel with the publishers, the prize culture and, latterly, what is being euphemised as the 'Amazon problem'. But we somehow suspect that these are only the tokens of a more intractable and elusive national malady. That there's something rotten about British culture that somehow fails to nourish the writing and reading of new fiction.

See, for example, the response of one writer, currently fêted in academic Europhile circles, who we voxpopped about new British fiction for this piece: 'I'm not sure I have anything to say. I didn't know there was any.' Disingenuous hauteur or self-possessed national self-dispossession? Is this now ritualised disavowal of the new in British fiction merely an empty but unexamined myth ripe for explosion, or are there real but more obstinate problems in nurturing innovative fictional writing in Britain? If so, do the problems lie with the writing, the perception of the writing, or with the national culture that frames production and reception of the writing? Or do the problems begin somewhere else altogether? Our refusenik jabbed his index finger at the problem and then shrugged his shoulders and walked away. Did he wish to deny his own status as an innovator, or his identity as British, or is he the self-styled exception that proves the rule?

In a culture where all too often literary 'innovation' is read as 'degeneration', where the experimental novelist is viewed as a case of narcissistic personality disorder, and where the new is identified with a 'creeping' cosmopolitanism that dilutes the local produce, the very idea of British innovative fiction comes to sound like an *oxymoronic* supplement – a kind of pharmakon – to the idea of the *moronic* inferno. Though postmodernism only ever reared its head disguised as a kind of indigenous contested empiricism – like arguments for the existence of the Loch Ness monster or Tony Blair's sincerity – its spectral afterlife is now source for lingering embarrassment within literary academia: pomo sold out, went commercial, went moronic, got down with the dodgier intimates of the inferno.

Academic literary critics attempting to push the case for a rejuvenated new British novel tend to sidestep the problem of the oxy and are anxious to avoid being tarred by the moronic. So they reframe the new in the terms of someplace or sometime or something else, most often the 'neo-modern' or the 'late modern' or the 'anxiously modern'. Or they have a field day with riffs on the 'new realism': hysterical, hyper–, contested, problematised, paranoid and dirty – but hardly ever *contemporary*. Peter Ackroyd wrote in 2001 about the way in which British novelists were now beginning to present reality as 'uncomfortable, as being demanding . . . less open to conventional habits of narration and description' and about how we are 'continually being made aware of the oddness of the ordinary, the menace and brutality which is behind the conventional political and social worlds'. Groping for a suitable nomenclature to append to the new writing, however, he ends lamely, albeit with characteristic disavowal of ownership: 'You might, I suppose, call it the new realism – paranoid realism.'

Soft–centred liberals all, we British seem shackled either to the safety of the readymade category, or the already canonised, or to the comfortably quotidian. Our peculiar creed is mortally suspicious of untrammelled aestheticism, endlessly asserting the primacy of content over form. In accounts of British writing, even now – long after such a thing could be anything other than a rather quaint anachronism of an old culture war – the avant–garde features as a kind of bogeyman. One whose dandified aestheticism belies a questionable politics, a moral compass gone awry; who must be beaten back by decency and common sense. Literary experiment still tends to be perceived as a pernicious form of French 'flu: of course we should still be *bloody grateful* for the English Channel, separating, as it does, steady, dependable old Blighty from *that kind of thing.*

A new, more 'patriotic' British citizenship test requires those seeking permanent residency in Britain to answer examination questions on Shakespeare, Dickens and Hardy. Without intending to revive that old chestnut of the British cultural studies of the eighties – all those debates about the national culture and the avowed 'greatness' of Shakespeare, Dickens and Hardy as Arnoldian touchstones of value – we still feel a kind of weary bafflement that official sanction should once again be given to the idea that learning a soundbite Shakespearian chakra might offer a quick route to cultural assimilation, or to what is considered most vigorous and most valuable about living in a new as well as an old country. Is this really the best they can do? A mercantilist visionary, a nineteenth–century Christian humanist, an agrarian *fin-de-siècle* melancholic?

But we no longer live even in an age of mechanical reproduction. We live in a post-industrial, neo-corporate, trans–national world of globalised forces where locating yourself in the particularities of a specific time and place requires more than rote learning the decontextualised soundbites of English literary tradition. Contemporary Britain, like the United States and the nations of Europe and Asia, is now a country with complex interconnections across the globe, through the circuits of international finance, the networks of the new corporate governance and management, and the social networks of the new media. Some of our newest fiction negotiates a path through this entanglement of the local and the global with exuberant style and an almost forensic eye for the way in which the experiential nuances of imagination, perception, memory and dream are all shaped by a culture, a place, a moment and memory. Shakespeare is not the only British inventor of New Worlds. If you were looking for the 'state of the nation' in British writing, you might put down HENRY V and set aside for a moment TESS OF THE D'URBERVILLES. You might, admittedly, linger over HARD TIMES, but you'd be better advised to turn to the occult histories of David Peace, for example, for their reflection of a nation struggling to come to terms with the very worst of its recent past, or to Nicola Barker, whose salty, Rabelaisian *bizarrerie* offers a truly democratic, and ordinarily strange, picture of Britain.

The British writer-critic James Wood, now distinguished Harvard professor and unacknowledged legislator of the fiefdom of contemporary fiction, has done much to consolidate the history of British literary fictional decline. Initially drawing useful ballast from Hugh Kenner's lament for a 'sinking island' after the demise of literary modernism, his transatlantic prognostications drew further scaffolding from postcolonial critics' version of the Great Aetiolation. Jed Esty has written the best-known account, but in framing it as yet another Empire Writes Back story, tethering the scope and preoccupations of the novel to shrinking Britain's post-imperial context, he places any reader in the inevitably compromised position of seeming, churlishly, to Write Back to an Empire That is Writing Back, and seeming, therefore, to collude with Empire. One of the official histories of the retreat from heroic, British ocean-going ambition, the Imperialist triumphalism anatomised in Conrad's HEART OF DARKNESS, Esty's account sees imperial greatness now stranded in a stagnant backwater, a kind of Kenneth Grahame messing about on the river, with Ratty, Badger and Mole, dabbling with the ducks in the safe rivulets of *English* pastoral. In this account, Forsterian lyrical realism established itself as *the* British Way of Fiction by turning British into English. Though Forster may have barely registered the sinking and the shrinkage of the nation in 1910, he noted all too well that its hub, its capital, floated vertiginously on a 'sea of porridge' thickened with foreign capital. Forster's answer was to exchange the hub for the heart and to recommend a quiet nativist retreat to the English Country House, the village pageant, with a dash of Pagan or Gothic mystery, and the occasional hint of German Romanticism.

Zadie Smith, kicking her heels on her way across the Atlantic, recently paid homage to the vision in her transatlantic novel, ON BEAUTY (2005), with its hard-won humanism and its belief in the redemptive power of art. A caricature, of course. Yet the Kenner-Wood-Esty case is curiously borne out in unlikely places. There is abundant evidence that our innovative writers – in a softer version of Eliotic European–Christian–Greco-Buddhist re-fashioning – have collaborated with it, seeming to need psychologically

E

to eschew the allegiances and associations of 'Britishness' or 'Englishness' and to assert the innovator aspect of their identities through self-conscious association with the Continental or the Transatlantic: one thinks here not only of Eliot's editorship of THE CRITERION, but of Murdoch's homage to Queneau and Beckett in her first novel; Trocchi and Brooke-Rose's love affair with French intellectual culture; Spark's with the Catholicism of Maritain rather than Newman; A. S. Byatt's avowal of herself as a European; Martin Amis's love-hate relationship with America and American writers such as Bellow and Roth; Zadie Smith's aforementioned looking back through the lens of all things cross-Atlantic (hip-hop and David Foster Wallace). Similar tendencies are evident in some of the most interesting and vigorous new writers such as Tom McCarthy, whose novels resonate with the Beckettian, the phenomenological and the existential, or in Alan Hollinghurst and Adam Thirlwell, who embrace an aristocratic, Euro-transatlantic lineage of James and Nabokov, Edmund White and Milan Kundera. Without exception, of course, all these self-avowedly 'cosmopolitan' writers marry with and promiscuously blend the foreign with the indigenous, the international with the demotic – but what seems to fix their identity in their own eyes and ours is their avowed association with cultures and traditions that are not British.

Some British writers seem to be getting over the hang up: they borrow and read and allude with ease to what Rushdie refers to as the 'sea of stories' and they write happily of the Isle of Dogs, of Shepperton, of Luton, the London Orbital, the East End, the lowlands and blackened wastelands of the industrialised Midlands, lives lived in back to back streets, on New Build Infotechland estates, remote Scottish islands, and the endless out-of-town shopping malls of the New Britain. This is a marked change from our parochial literary past. Take for example Kazuo Ishiguro's oft-pronounced sense of the difficulties of escaping the provincialism of British fiction in the seventies, the feeling of Britain's increasing marginalisation in world-politics, a geographic isolationism so evident that it seemed impossible to imagine that literary value could not be part of the general 'shrinkage'. British writers felt that the Big Events were happening elsewhere; interesting fiction was bound to follow; the balance of powers was shifting.

His own novel THE UNCONSOLED of 1996 was a brilliant rendition of the dangers and seductions of 'going International' as a way of escaping this threat of parochialism (interestingly also the theme too of Adam Thirlwell's more recent novel of that name). Ishiguro's THE UNCONSOLED is a psychomachia of the newly professionalised cosmopolitan artist struggling to maintain a fierce public relations 'schedule' with pressures on him to perform his art and exercise a telescopic ambassadorial philanthropy. On yet another tour, he finds himself in a strange space of nowhere, an international hotel, in an unnamed place, at an unnamed time, somewhere in the middle of Europe. He wrestles too with a landscape awash with material projections

of his own autobiographical memories, fantasies, dreams and fears. Surely a figure
for the new professionalised and internationalised writer, Ryder bumps up against the
ghosts of his past and the buried and split-off alters of himself, in a landscape built out
of hints and glimpses of THE WASTE LAND, Ariadne on Naxos, Escher's drawings, the
films of Bergman and the Coen brothers, German Romanticism, Nietzsche and Freud,
the traditions of the Mittel-European volk.

Similarly, literary modernism, which for so many years was the straw man of
a British distrust of intellectualism, has in recent times seen its stock rise. On the
publication of last year's UMBRELLA, Will Self confessed that for all his previous ex-
cursions into the demotic and the grotesque, he'd really always been a closet modernist.
UMBRELLA, he says, with its four hundred pages of unbroken stream of consciousness,
is the book he wanted to write all along. Self's belated coming out is a measure of the
extent to which the prejudices that were rife amongst modernism's first- and second-
generation legatees – C. P. Snow, Kingsley Amis, The Movement poets et al. – had
persisted well into the closing decades of the twentieth century. That stereotype of
modernism as a toothless old crone comfortably installed, decades before, at the centre
of Establishment good taste and none-too-threatening when busied with manifesting
fevered daydreams of some prelapsarian Edwardian past – but all too susceptible
to fifth columnist tendencies – was not easily shifted. As late as 1992, John Carey's
THE INTELLECTUALS AND THE MASSES conspiracy-theorised the modern's apparent
systematic and pre-meditated attack on mass culture.

Now, after the fag end of pomo, modernism seems to be having a moment. As the
early years of the twenty-first century categorically fail to deliver anything like the
extraordinary flowering of artistic energies that emerged during the first decades of
the twentieth, writers and critics (and publishers, with all the entrepreneurial spirit of
the original Moderns) are beginning to reinvest in modernism's achievements. In some
cases, it's being reinvented anew on the same terms as the old prejudices, welcomed
back as modernism-without-the-menaces, thoroughly domesticised and with the sting
of literary experimentation removed – Smith's ON BEAUTY we've already mentioned,
but see also Alan Hollinghurst's THE LINE OF BEAUTY. Ian McEwan famously
declared against the 'dead hand of modernism', in fear, presumably, of that avant-
garde bogeyman, as if, as China Miéville has commented, 'the dominant literary mode
in postwar England was Steinian experimentation or some Albion Oulipo'. But even
McEwan has written a 'modernist' novel, ATONEMENT – if only to indict and rewrite
modernism for its dereliction of duty.

For others, however, it's being returned to as an unfinished project, as a funda-
mental turning point that British culture, ostrich-like as ever, seems to have missed.
Gabriel Josipovici's recent *kulturpessimismus* polemic, WHAT EVER HAPPENED TO
MODERNISM? (2010) condemns a buttoned-up Englishry that he sees as dreary and

anecdotal, unable to distinguish between reality and *l'effet de réel*; one that has consistently misunderstood the modernist project. To ignore the avant-garde, says Tom McCarthy, whose own critical success as a novelist is testament to a renewed appetite for modernism, 'is the equivalent of ignoring Darwin'. But about the novels yielded by this twenty-first-century modernist impulse – Self's *UMBRELLA* and McCarthy's own *C*, for example, which have been breathlessly heralded as a kind of modernism *après la lettre* – there is something of the Sealed Knot. These are, inevitably, not modernist novels as such (and how could they be?) but novels *about* modernism. Ones that adopt its pre-existing codes, tropes and conventions for the sake of nostalgia – which, it bears repeating, doth not modernism make. The category of modernism, ever loose to the point of unwieldy, increasingly seems to mean a 'better class' (read: borrowed from the –isms of the European avant-garde) of literary allusion. Or it is deployed merely to denote a sense of solidity, of seriousness, of authenticity, or of difficulty.

For Josipovici, what has been crucially ignored by British book culture is the ways in which modernism represents the 'coming into awareness by art of its precarious status and responsibilities' and will therefore 'from now on, always be with us'. Thing is, to a certain extent, it always has. Josipovici, McCarthy and co. seem to be relying upon the same bowdlerised version of British literary history as their adversaries. In fact, part of the problem for the serious literary novelist in Britain has actually often been the difficulty of getting over modernism. Not just as a problem of production, but one of reception too. The new experimental writer was once almost inevitably going to be dubbed the new Beckett or Kafka or Joyce. Once modernism was set up as introspective and concerned with the 'dark places of psychology', to use Woolf's description, writers of the forties like Green, Bowen and Compton-Burnett saw the challenge as finding a way to eschew the assumed 'inward turn' in order to create worlds through dialogue, expressionist rendition, behaviourist technique and phenomenologies of perception that blurred memory and perception, inner and outer voices, hierarchies of narration.

Crucial to this was the intuitive novelistic recognition (spelt out later, philosophically, by both Sartre and Merleau-Ponty) already powerful in Bowen and Green, that feeling is not always, most often not in fact, felt; feeling is most often experienced as the feeling-tone or mood that seems more the attribute of a world or a scene: the vibrancy of backlighting, shadows, edges, colours, the rhythm and pace of a world made in words. Perception is style, as Martin Amis has insisted, but perception is also style that unconceals, tacitly and obliquely, a world and, through a process of reverse introjection, a self. That the world exists for me as my world and that I exist for myself, is what Sartre refers to as *ipseity*. The feeling that I don't exist, the loss of a tacit sense of self-presence, that I don't inhabit my body or the world, is the feeling-tone pervasive in fiction since the seventies but first captured as part of a

E

new inhospitable and corporate world in Camus' THE STRANGER. Meursault cannot feel at all, but his world is conveyed through one of the most powerful and distinctive 'feeling-tones' in modern fiction (Amis, incidentally, uses the word in TIME'S ARROW in a similar attempt to write the Nazi soul). This mode of disconnection in its blank, or hyper-reflexive, or comically disjunctive form – that begins with Dostoevsky, Kafka, Musil and Beckett – has been a major orientation of twentieth-century literary fiction in Britain, but is barely remarked upon in the general preoccupation with making fine discriminations between realism and modernism and late modernism and postmodernism.

It is the very self-consciously executed modus vivendi of McCarthy's REMAINDER. Take the WATT-like scene with the carrot in the physiotherapy clinic:

> 'I closed my fingers round the carrot. It felt – well, it felt; that was enough to start short-circuiting the operation. It had texture; it had mass. The whole week I'd been gearing up to lift it, I'd thought of my hands, my fingers, my rerouted brain as active agents, and the carrot as a nothing – a hollow, a carved space for me to grasp and move. This carrot though, was more active than me: the way it bumped and wrinkled; how it crawled with grit.'

Like Ryder, this protagonist is another who conceives of himself as an artist; this novel too – like Ishiguro's NEVER LET ME GO or Hilary Mantel's BEYOND BLACK or Hollinghurst's less overtly experimental THE LINE OF BEAUTY or Smith's ON BEAUTY – is a disquisition on the place of art in a commodified world.

Here a Platonic intentionality – but it could as well be romantic – attempts to materialise its vision through various corporate networks of facilitation and, in the process, exposes the dangerous and mechanistic splitting of mind, body and world that lurks in the Platonic and the Cartesian and is now generalised over Britain in the corporate world of reality management. McCarthy's twenty-first century Frankenstein inhabits and acts out a hyper-reflexive world of 'cool' where money is able to hire an army of networked agents, project managers and special-effects workers specialised in the materialisation of corporate 'vision' as the already confabulated memories viewed as the remaining source of the idea of a soul. Like Ishiguro's, McCarthy's novel too is also about fiction as compensation – a settlement – that undoes itself as it points up all those losses and holes in the real. It is a world where performance is all, and weariness, the weariness of the self, has long set in; where a Beckettian akrasia is now a circuit-disconnect between wiring and neurotransmission in the brain and wiring and neurotransmission to the muscles of the body. It is a world where the pre-reflexive has been almost entirely replaced by the management of the event and the orchestrated confabulation of the 'real' as memory, dream and perception.

E

REMAINDER has made its mark, perhaps, because it so exquisitely connects the metafictional with the neo–corporate with our revived interest in the phenomenology of perception and imagination and feeling. How does a novelist preserve the anagnosia that is at the heart of practical daily living, the tacit knowing that eludes language? How do you do it in words? And how do you use those words to expose a world where words have been betrayed into the service of a coercive management and production of a kind of emptied out real: the new management protocols of event production, performance monitoring and the corporate scripting of the real as 'cool'? Perhaps the really new realism is that we turn to fiction to experience the feeling of the real. Maybe it's to this that James Wood refers when he defines 'novelistic intelligence' as the capacity to invoke the 'reachably real'. Maybe he's not just propounding the rightful function of the novel as merely fictional shadow–play. But somehow we doubt it. Nonetheless, this takes us somehow beyond the postmodern.

In our obsessions with modernism, postmodernism, realism, neomodernism, late modernism, the hysterical, the paranoid, the hyper– and the ever 'new' realism, perhaps we have forgotten that a major strength of the British novel has always lain in this kind of phenomenological, often semi–expressionist rendition and self–conscious rehearsal of the building and dismantling of imaginary worlds and the fabulation of a sense of the real. It is there in Sterne's ironic laying bare of the sentimentalist claims for the novel at the beginning of the era of political economy, or in Woolf's dissemination of mind through the complex representation of phenomenologies of perception, memory and imagination, or in Muriel Spark's wicked way of estranging us from our lived and assumed modes of estrangement as she takes a willed detour round the sentimental to restore us to a proper empathy with the poor, the marginalised and excluded.

Without this altered perception of literary history, the fifties will continue to be written up as a disappointing and unambitious return to or collapse back into middle–of–the–road social realism: ignoring the surrealism of A. L. Barker, the comic and haunting expressionism of late Green, the hyper–reflexive strangeness of Rex Warner's THE AERODROME, the Tourettish and grotesque mimicry that makes up much of Amis' LUCKY JIM, the Wittgensteinian reflection on and enaction of solipsism that is William Golding's PINCHER MARTIN, the dispersed, disconnected consciousness that engages the experience of factory life in Sillitoe's SATURDAY NIGHT AND SUNDAY MORNING, or the comic suburban grotesque of William Sansom's brilliant novel, THE BODY. Writers such as Beryl Bainbridge, Doris Lessing, early McEwan, Murdoch, Spark, Ballard, Kelman, Burgess, all cut their teeth as part of this trajectory; the legacy extends to McCarthy, Barker, Peace, Self and many others.

To accept this alternative picture is surely to take on board the possibility that there are outward–looking but native traditions of experiment that exceed the usual

E

accounts of the so-called inward turn of modernism, or the turning inside out of fictional convention in the postmodern, or the insider–outsider, Empire Writes Back, double perspectivism of the post-colonial. There is a native version of phenomenology and it flourishes in our fiction; surrealism, expressionism and blankness rub along with comic extravagance, linguistic exuberance and a Todorovian kind of fantastic, happily mingling natural with supernatural and the spiritual and transcendental with the weird and wacky. A kind of British *bizarrerie*.

Yet, the story of the decline of the nation tacked onto the fortunes of the novel, the academic obsession with historical and stylistic placing and categorisation, even a kind of lingering Leavisism that sees art primarily as a guide to the moral or the good life, all create problems for the perception, reception and encouragement of aesthetic newness in Britain. The self-induced dispossession of national identity so marked in our literary culture seems, well, *British*. And it often feels remarkably difficult to avoid the self-fulfilling pressure of the stereotype. Turn to the American writer Jonathan Franzen's recent apologia for his own style of autobiographical fiction, for example, and there's no hint of such identity problems: 'When I write,' he says, 'I don't feel like a craftsman influenced by earlier craftsmen who were themselves influenced by earlier craftsmen. I feel like a member of a single, large virtual community in which I have dynamic relationships with other members of the community, most of whom are no longer living. As in any other community, I have my friends and I have my enemies. I find my way to the corners of the world of fiction where I feel most at home, most securely but also provocatively among my friends.' Franzen's place is comfortably globetrotting round the worlds of fiction in his head: the world of fiction as a world of story-worlds and not promotional tours, publicity launches and national book culture.

But a question remains, perhaps, whether there was actually a falling off during many and various periods which commentators have identified as their literary *annus horribilis*. In a now infamous 1993 editorial to the literary magazine GRANTA, Bill Buford blamed the word 'British' itself for poisoning the wells of talent: 'a grey, unsatisfactory, bad-weather kind of word, a piece of linguistic compromise'. In a landscape (then) beginning to seem more refreshed by the voices of the trans-national, the migrant and the diasporic, the idea of 'British', however, for Buford, seemed to hang in the air like a toxic miasma, stymieing progress and the cultivation of the new. 'British' was a bad spell; no longer a description of the real. 'I still don't know anyone who is British. I know people who are English or Scottish or Northern Irish (not to mention born in Nigeria but living here or born-in-London of Pakistani parents and living here ... or born-in-Nigeria-but-living-here-Nigerian-English).' But Buford too (also an American) now seems strangely hung up on the Kenner account, convinced that the only means of renewal still depended on Imperial powers, now in reverse as the Empire Wrote Back.

Though there is no necessary connection between the luminosity of events in history and the significance and value of artistic representation, literary critics seem curiously attached to this view of things. They are driven perhaps by different concerns than writers themselves, concerns to do with historical placing, cultural trajectories, political interventions, real or imagined, and less so with the nitty–gritty of that incredibly difficult task of imagining and making a world. If we literary critics thought more like novelists and less like historians or sociologists, perhaps we might begin to see that the fifties consisted of more than Angry Young Men or deferential genuflections in bicycle clips. Perhaps we might begin to do justice to the immensely variegated and innovatory work of that decade and perhaps we might see the fifties is a good place to begin to explode the Kenner and Co. myth of inevitable decline? Similarly, perhaps, the 1980s had more on offer than a political imagination fired up by Margaret Thatcher or the Empire Writing Back or Lyotard's critique of metanarratives. Perhaps even the 1970s, as the Age of No Style, had styles that awaited a hermeneutic imagination more attuned to factories than flares, ghosts than governments, Granny rock than Glam rock (Beryl Bainbridge's *THE BOTTLE FACTORY OUTING* perhaps as against Martin Amis's *THE PREGNANT WIDOW*).

Writers are freer than critics to ignore the strictures of periodisation, the interminable debates about location and positioning. They can stick their necks out more freely – aren't they meant to? – without alienating an 'interpretive community' or being excluded from the academic Research Exercise – the six yearly cull of academic 'research' imposed by a national government stingy on higher education funding but generous to the point of silliness with the provision of League Tables:

> I've never understood the categorisation of postcolonial writing. I've been sent papers where I'm talked about as a postcolonial novelist, but I'm never sure about the definition. Does "postcolonial" mean writing that came out in the postcolonial era? Or does it have to come from a country that used to be part of an empire, and which, after the colonies started to devolve, changed into an independent state? Or does it mean writing by people who don't have white skins ... Whether somebody is postcolonial seems to be defined by the writer's biography rather than by their writing, and that's what makes me very suspicious of postcolonial writing as a category.

Ishiguro voices something often obscurely felt but ne'er so well expressed – or, more likely, ne'er dared to be expressed, at least by academic critics forced to keep one eye on political and the other on professional correctness. What if novels are primarily now read as ways out of loneliness, as Jonathan Franzen has recently averred? Does that make them less difficult to write? Or less political? Doesn't that entail trying to understand and find ways to represent, analyse and imaginatively transform the sources of our sense of contemporary disaffection or lack of or skewed affect? Historicisation in fiction is rooted in the singularity of a story world, created through a process of formal imagination and craft. If we make fiction 'piggyback' too much on history, as Ishiguro suggests later in the same interview (2012), 'it leads to the preservation of mediocre books whilst some brilliant books are forgotten because they don't fit the clear historical model.' We've persisted in drawing upon a textbook version of literary history, at the expense of engaging fully with the realities of literary practice. And insofar as such a model ever could anywhere, the one that bisects the twentieth century more-or-less down the middle, dividing its paper assets between the categories of modernism and postmodernism – drawing a discreet veil over a mid-century 'return to realism' which we prefer not to talk about – has never comfortably applied here. Sometimes new mutations, hopeful monsters, struggling to push their way out of blighted soil are trodden over by the love affair with historical frames or correctness.

Yet, despite the successive incursions of threads, pockets and outcroppings of the experimental and the reality of a more variegated literary history than 'official' accounts almost always offer, the mainstream picture of the British novel is still dominated by the idea of a time-worn 'English style'. Colm Tóibín recently characterised the 'quintessential English novel of our age' as 'well made, low on ambition and filled with restraint, taking its bearings from a world that Philip Larkin made in his own image'. Zadie Smith, in her essay 'Two Paths for the Novel' speculates on the future of fiction in English by way of reviews of novels by latter-day realist, Joseph O'Neill, and of Tom McCarthy as the great hope for British avant-garde writing. She finds O'Neill's is the road most travelled. His 'breed of lyrical realism' (there we go again) has 'had the freedom of the highway for some time now, with most other exits blocked'. Although Smith specifies the Anglophone novel, her view seems more narrowly applicable to fiction in Britain. At the Edinburgh Writer's Conference last year, China Miéville spoke of the English novel's 'remorseless prioritisation ... of recognition over estrangement'. The timeliness of Ali Smith's revival of the old literary chestnut of style versus content at the same event is perhaps testament to the paucity of our thinking about what novels are and what they can do.

We've had the good grace to export this ethic in the views of James Wood, 'the finest literary critic writing in English today' (as is customary to append). His pleas for reason and decency against a pervasive American fetish for vulgar stylistics, for those 'very "brilliant" books which know a thousand things but do not know a single human being', issue weekly from the pages of the NEW YORKER. For in Britain, where, as we've seen, the state of the novel is more likely to be closely pegged to the state of the nation, fiction has been obliged to provide a repository for stable truths and social order. 'Englishness' (very rarely 'Britishness') has remained a major preoccupation in our fictions. Novels have long been burdened with providing the sense of spiritual coherence that social commentators insist we so sorely lack despite, or, in fact, because of, an increasingly dispersed and devolved national culture.

Last year, the summer of the British monarch's Diamond Jubilee and the London Olympics tested an uneasy, class conscious, and ambivalent relationship with a nationalism reinterpreted as national pride and belonging that many British people are still loathe to admit. Those celebrations followed on from the previous summer's outbreak of violence, raids, looting and riots that saw major areas of the city of London in flames. Interspersed with BBC coverage of Wimbledon, a new Shakespeare season and pictures of the Olympic torch on its progress round the towns of Britain were documentaries and narratives of the mostly 16–24 year-old rioters now released from prison and facing life with disabling criminal convictions. As for nationalism, as Stefan Collini writes, we seem always to have insisted that such a primitive – and historically troublesome – impulse is something that happens elsewhere. The issue has long been a vexed one here. The World War II-era injunction to 'Keep Calm and Carry On' has become the atavistic mantra of Recession Britain visible everywhere from towels to teacups. It appeals to our mythic image of ourselves; the 'blitz spirit' with which we might weather this new Age of Austerity. But as our 'collective symbol' the Union Jack has an uncomfortable double existence. It is similarly, 'harmless' pageantry, a Little England party favour, but it is also historically loaded and queasily evocative, making us instinctively – and often unquestioningly – uneasy.

We have not lost our mania for manifesting the particularity (and the peculiarity) of being English. The metaphysics of Eliot and Leavis might have gone lukewarm for many and stone cold for most, but we still continue to attempt to conjure a coherent whole from less than the sum of its parts. But the smoggy mill towns, red pillar boxes and fried breakfasts of an English particularist like Orwell have, however, given way to rather more ersatz assemblages. The cover of last year's Britain-themed issue of GRANTA depicts a chipped bone china teacup with its handle wrenched off. This, neatly, is the 'Broken Britain' of tabloid and Tory parlance. The nation recorded within is peopled with desperate pen-pushers, small-time dealers of recreational pharmaceuticals, missing children, Eastern European lap dancers and timorous lower-league footballers with Lady Chatterley-esque designs upon the groundsman. It's an urban-pastoral hinterland, hung with a murder-scene gloaming of incipient menace. Abandoned old-New Towns and sink estates, the condemned edifices of post-war utopian dreaming – and of local government corruption – feature heavily. So, too, does a British state of mind governed by shame, repression and lassitude and given to random and not-so-random acts of violence.

Yet it is with these ingredients, the poet and novelist John Burnside argues,

E

that we might put Britain, like Humpty Dumpty, back together again. '[H]ome, or identity,' he suggests, 'can be found in cultural ruins.' Britain might be, as self-styled alternative poet laureate Simon Armitage has it, reduced to a 'shipwreck's carcass' and 'down to its bare bones', but with the loss of 'old certainties' comes the loosening of the old hierarchies too, and with it the possibility for remodelling Britain along more democratic, more egalitarian lines. This, for Burnside, is cause for a 'tender, if guarded, celebration':

> To recognise the new values that emerge from the makeshift is to discover the earliest traces of a new direction, the first tentative steps in a spontaneous remaking of ourselves, the hazy outline of a democratising order that imagination finds in the unlikeliest of places.

But is this really the cause for (albeit cautious) jubilation? Should a 'sense of identity' really come at such a cost? And is celebration really the most appropriate response? GRANTA's picture of Britain is not, as it purports to be, an unflinchingly democratic picture of a diverse society, but the finessing of a poverty of many kinds into the picturesque; the requisite local colour now provided by all those on-the-bones-of-their-arse Britons.

Burnside seems at once to under- and over-estimate what art can do. We might now be rather more sceptical about the real-world capabilities of the artistic imagination to ameliorate social injustice. And we might question how effective a model of egalitarianism narrative fiction can be. The iconography of this 'Broken Britain' is well on its way to becoming a collection of clichés of 'Englishness' that is just as politically malign, cosy and self-satisfied than the old one. Burnside's is, at least, a very British sentiment: It might be *crap* but at least it's *ours*. For Martin Amis, on the other hand, the appropriate response to a country he recently declaimed for its 'moral decrepitude' is satire. Last year's 'State of England' novel, *LIONEL ASBO*, is a parting shot as Amis absconds for America. 'Who let the dogs in?' the epigraph asks, in the first of many woefully misjudged (and woefully out-of-date) pop culture references. In the novel, Amis romances Britain's underclass into a coterie of grotesques that are at once Jerry Springer-generic and farcically bizarre: the single mothers, illiterate bruisers and petty criminals are joined by a glamour model-slash-aspiring poetess, pitbulls raised on Tabasco. The response has been almost unanimously negative; unsurprising since, as once reviewer commented, Amis's novel amounts to little more than narrative-as-trolling.

Fellow novelist Nicola Barker has been a rare voice in defence of *LIONEL ASBO*, arguing, in her review, that 'maybe modern England needs offending'. She maintains that thin-skinned Britons might well need this kind of baiting to shake them from their cosy, tea–and–biscuits slumber. Surprising, this, from Barker, since although she was recently puffed as the 'female Martin Amis', her own novels engage with the 'reality' of living in Britain (*whatever that might mean*, her fictions always insist on appending) with an authenticity and a sensitivity rarely seen in Amis's. Far from proffering a searing critique of the state of the nation, Barker's so–called progenitor appears to be in cahoots with a culture that is, in terms of its cruelty and vacuity, already way beyond the poison of his pen. See for example, the ritualised humiliations of über–franchised reality television or even more so our government, whose economic policymaking in the face of the global economic recession evinces a level of care and sympathy more often seen in the S&M parlour, or indeed, in the public school fagging system with which Prime Minister David Cameron is so familiar. 'We' (who, *us*?) have been decadent, chastise the swingeing cuts initiated by the coalition government, and now, inevitably, *we must be punished*.

It is customary, at this juncture, to segue effortlessly into tentative optimism. To defer to the 'complexity' of the situation. To issue disclaimers about the partial view of our presentism. To talk of 'green shoots' and 'possibilities'. This piece, in a sense, is no exception. We suggest that what afflicts the British novel might not be as elusive as it seems. That the problem, in fact, might lie closer to home.

Literary criticism, once envisioned by F. R. Leavis as the 'humane centre' of British culture, long since split into the factions of Grub Street and Ivory Tower, and there has been little love lost between the two since Leavis's heyday. Reacting against this ethical burden, the British literary academy was a keen late adapter to continental theory. Over–eager, in fact; for it was soon accused by novelists of having all but abandoned the novel, having thrown the baby out with the bath water of Leavis and the New Criticism. This caricature of academe is, at least in part, the product of a long–standing British mistrust of 'Theory'. Yet who could blame literary academics for sexing up the British novel with liberal applications of cool, continental philosophy on hot topics like death and desire; or those who manage to divine an encounter with the Lacanian Real in the po–faced sex–farce (sometimes labelled 'neo–Victorian') of Ian McEwan's ON CHESIL BEACH? But in this era of impact–assessment and quota–fulfilment, the academy's attempts to grapple with the British contemporary novel have often felt like a will–this–do concession to relevance. Perhaps it would be better advised to modify its attempts to validate its objects of study by overburdening them with demands for relevance to political or government correctness and simply try to lift the longstanding taboo on aesthetic evaluation that might lend its weight to, well, better novels.

The literary press in Britain has eagerly taken up the Leavisite slack, moonlighting as the moral advocate of the self–consciously middlebrow. It exists as the heavily–subsidised, loss–making adjuncts and supplements to newspapers, with the exception of the LONDON REVIEW OF BOOKS, funded by its editor's family trust. Perhaps because of this, as with so much cultural life in Britain, our literary press is all too aware of a public service remit, but is by no means sure of whom its audience might comprise. It addresses an Ideal Reader that is both unapologetically philistine and impossibly highfalutin'. That likes its books 'serious' and 'weighty', but not 'dry' or 'obscure' and certainly never to 'lack heart'. That wants its ethical heuristics trussed up in majestically lyrical prose.

Whilst British literary critics are reverential about the innate value of the (definite article, capital letter) Novel, they remain wholly unconvinced about the broader poss-ibilities of fictional narrative. See, for example, Liam McIlvanney and Ray Ryan's take on the 'novelness' of novels in THE GOOD OF THE NOVEL (2011):

> One can say, for one thing, that the truth of novels cannot be rendered in any other form; it cannot be abstracted or codified, turned into thesis or proposition. Novelistic truth is not data, not reportage, not documentary, not philosophical tenet, not political slogan. Novelistic truth is dramatic, which means above all it has to do with character ... In exploring character, the novel's key strength is the disclosure of human interiority. To the question, what does the novel do?, we might most pertinently answer: the novel does character, and the novel does interiority.

Character and interiority; no mention here of the novel's capacity not just to 'disclose' but to expand the remit of human experience, for instance, to offer temporary access to other ways of perceiving. Or of the novel as thought experiment, as a viable form of knowledge all of its own – let alone as a ticket to peak experience at the limits of language. Here – where novels are breathlessly praised for their skilful navigation of our twenty-first century dilemmas and for the delicate craft of their storytelling – lies what used to be called literary fiction in Britain. E. M. Forster need not have worried about the fate of his 'little society' – it is alive and well, at least in the pages of the literary press.

Until the 1970s, new and innovative British fiction could at least count upon its allies in publishing. Back then, 'good' books were safeguarded by the support and patronage of swashbuckling, semi-mythical publishing mavericks like John Calder, Marion Boyars and Tom Maschler. Now, in these dark days for the book industry, as the novelist Deborah Levy has commented, 'There is no way you can send a fierce, exotic and brutally truthful hothead novel out into the British rain in a recession and expect a deal to be on the table with scones, tea and the DAILY MAIL.' New books are subject to the bottom line of multinational publishing conglomerates which are rationalising and prioritising as never before. Even the braver editors have the jitters, unwilling to take a punt on those books deemed untested and unmarketable. To emerge from the slush pile now, novels must meet cynical editorial policies which attempt to second guess, on the one hand, the whims of the market by trying to appease some phantasmic lowest common denominator and, on the other, the vagaries of literary prize culture by seeking to appeal to some gold standard of literary 'good taste'. And, overall, insist on radically underestimating the appetites of the British reading public. This, then, is the British literary establishment. The perfect pricks, so to speak, to kick against. Or, so you might think. But, in fact, a book counterculture in Britain has been slow to emerge. There are exceptions, without doubt: this very magazine, of course, the newish press And Other Stories, for example, who enjoyed early success with Levy's SWIMMING HOME, the imprint Faber Finds, which is making efforts to put right the wrongs of literary history, and others. But still the little magazines, periodicals and presses of other books cultures (and of poetry) do not exist in such significant numbers here. Tellingly, when the OBSERVER recently profiled the thriving lit mag scene, it looked to New York and to n+1, TRIPLE CANOPY and the NEW INQUIRY.

In fact, in Britain, increasingly there's the sense that new and innovative fiction is beginning to abscond from the realm of the strictly 'literary' altogether, and is making for the sunnier and more welcoming climes of the art world. See, for example, the Semina series of experimental texts edited by writer and artist Stewart Home, published by Bookworks, an independent art publisher. Or Visual Editions, which seeks to draw together the art book and the literary text to publish what they call 'visual writing' like Adam Thirlwell's KAPOW! and Jonathan Safran Foer's TREE OF CODES, alongside a new edition of what is perhaps the ur-text of the experimental novel, TRISTRAM SHANDY. Will the art world, then, provide a place for innovative writing to flourish in Britain? Can a home be found for this ailing medium in a milieu that is less hamstrung by misplaced moral and ethical obligations and the strictures of the marketplace (both real and imaginary) and, significantly, is better funded?

And where might this leave British book culture? Despite their differences, writer, critic and academic alike find themselves under threat and compromised – economically and existentially – by the re-structuring and re-development of the new globalised neo-corporatisms, with their token nods to green recycling and New Age recovery, and their sinister and often systematic appropriations of everything from art to the social network to the 'event'. The work of art exists no longer in a romantic-modernist age of mechanical reproduction but in the disseminated and pervasive global networks of the neo-corporate and the new knowledge economy. Being 'local' is unavoidably a way of being 'global'; getting inside the singular consciousness may be less a business of flowing along a stream of consciousness than evoking a structure of feeling of a world that, as Musil discerned long ago, is filling up with men without qualities, men incorporated into the neo-corporate spaces of the new knowledge economy. If postmodernism was a lament for depths lost to late consumer capital,

E

it was always easy prey to charges of mendacious and slippery complicity with the enemy. If we are currently now officially in an 'interregnum', past the post and into a new age of 're' — redevelopment, recycling, restructuring, reparation, reconciliation, residue, remainder, remembrance, recession — trying to rebuild foundations, recover roots and re-imagine a future re-connected with a revisioned past, we are also being forced to acknowledge how far past the post we are in other ways too — poised uncertainly but apocalyptically on the brink of environmental disaster and economic collapse. Artistically and imaginatively, though British and stranded on a sinking island, we too inhabit the new world of the globalised and the neo-corporate frozen style that deploys its resources in the professional management and production of the real. There is, quite discernibly, a new climate of seriousness, a sense of 'growing up' from postmodernism, but the abatement of fears about the death of the author by no means presents new death-threats to the artistic imagination. Innovative and ambitious novels certainly continue to be written in Britain; there might be more of them, and those that there are might be better known, if only there was someone to vouch for them.

TALIA CHETRIT

CHILDREN OF GOD

BY

PETER STAMM

(*tr.* MICHAEL HOFMANN)

IT WAS THE FIRST MICHAEL had heard of the girl. His housekeeper was telling him about her: she claimed – Mandy did – that there was no father. She lived in the neighbouring village of W. The housekeeper laughed, Michael sighed. As if it wasn't enough that church attendance was way down, that the old people sent him away when he tried to visit them in their home, and the children cheeked him in Sunday school. It was all Communism, he said, or the after-effects of it. Ach, nonsense, said the housekeeper, it was never any different. Did he know the large sugar-beet field on the road to W.? There was a sort of island in the middle of it. A clump of trees had been left standing by the farmer. Since forever, she said. And that's where he has assignations with a woman. What woman? asked Michael. What farmer? The one who's there, and his father before him, and his grandfather before that. All of them. Since forever. We're only human, after all, them and me. Each of us has his needs.

Michael sighed. He had been the minister here since spring, but he hadn't got any closer to his flock. He came from the mountains, where everything was different: the people, the landscape, and the sky, which here was so infinitely wide and remote.

She claims she's never been with a man, said the housekeeper, the baby must be a gift from God. That Mandy girl, she said, was the daughter of Gregor who works for the bus company. The little fat driver. He gave her a good spanking, she was black and blue all over. And now the whole village is scratching its head over who the father might be. There aren't a lot of men living there who are candidates. Maybe it was Marco the landlord. Or a passing tramp. She's no oil painting, you know. But you take what you can get. That Mandy, she's not the brightest either, said the housekeeper: maybe she didn't realise. Up on the ladder picking cherries. All right, all right, said Michael.

❡ Mandy came to the vicarage while Michael was eating lunch. The housekeeper brought her in, and he asked her to sit down and talk to him. She just sat there with downcast eyes and didn't speak. She smelled of soap. Michael ate, and kept sneaking looks at the young woman. She wasn't pretty, but she wasn't ugly either. Perhaps she would turn to fat later. Now she was plump. She's blooming, thought Michael. And he sneaked a look at her belly and her big breasts, very prominent under the rather garish sweater. He didn't know if it was pregnancy or food. Then the young woman looked at him and immediately lowered her eyes, and he pushed away his half-eaten lunch and stood up. Let's go out in the garden.

The year was far along. The leaves were turning on the trees. The morning had been misty, now the sun was trying to break through. Michael and Mandy walked together in the garden. Your Reverence, she said, and he, No, please just call me Michael, and I'll call you Mandy. So she didn't know who the father was? There was no father, said Mandy, I never... She stopped. Michael sighed. Sixteen, eighteen, he thought, no older than that. My dear child, he said, it's a sin, but God will forgive you. Thus saith the Lord God of Israel: Every bottle shall be filled with wine!

Mandy tore a leaf off the old linden tree where they had come to a stop, and Michael said, Do you know how it is when a man lies with a woman? You mean, with the peter, said Mandy, and she blushed and looked down. Perhaps it was in her sleep, thought Michael, apparently such things happen. They had studied it in school, Mandy added, and quickly: Erection, coitus, and rhythm method. All right, all right, said Michael, school. That was the upshot of having so many Communists still sitting on school boards.

Holy mother of God, said Mandy, I've never... All right, all right, said Michael, and then, with sudden vehemence, Well, where do you think the baby's come from then? Do you think it's a gift from God? Yes, said Mandy. He sent her home.

❡ On Sunday, Michael saw Mandy among the few who were at the service. If he remembered correctly, she had never been before. She was wearing a simple dress in dark green, and now he could see her condition plainly. She should be ashamed of herself, said the housekeeper.

Mandy was all at sea. Michael could see her craning around. When the others sang, she didn't. And when she came forward at the end to receive Communion, he had to tell her, Open your mouth.

Michael spoke about steadiness in adversity. Frau Schmidt, who was always there, read the lesson with a quiet but firm voice. See that ye refuse not him that speaketh. For if they escaped not who refused him that spake on earth: be not forgetful to entertain strangers: for thereby some have entertained angels unawares.

Michael had kept his eyes closed during the reading, and he felt he could almost see the angel who came to visit men, an angel that had Mandy's face, and whose belly in its white robes bulged like Mandy's in her dress. Suddenly it got very quiet in the church. Michael opened his eyes and saw that everyone was looking at him expectantly. Then he said: We can speak with confidence. The Lord is my helper, and I will not fear what man shall do unto me.

After the service was over, Michael hurried over to the door to see out his old biddies. He had shut the door behind the last of them when he saw that Mandy was kneeling at the altar. He went up to her and laid his hand on her head. She looked at him, and he saw she had tears running down her cheeks. Come, he said, and he led her out of the church and across the road to the cemetery. Look at all these people, he said, they were all sinners: but God took them to Himself, and He will forgive you your sins as well. I am full of sin, said Mandy, but I have never been with a man. All right, all right, said Michael, and he touched Mandy's shoulder with his hand.

F

But when he touched Mandy, it was as though his heart and his whole body were filling with a joy he had never felt in his life, and he shrank back, as though he had burned himself. And if it's true? he thought.

¶ And if it's true? he thought that afternoon, as he walked down the road to the next village. The sun was shining and the sky was wide and cloudless. Michael felt tired after lunch, but his heart was still filled with the joy that had flowed from Mandy's body into his own: and if it's true?

He often walked to one of the other villages on a Sunday afternoon, striding quickly down the tree-lined roads in rain or shine. But on that day he had an objective. He had called the doctor who lived there, a man by the name of Klaus, and asked if he might talk to him: no, he couldn't tell him what about.

Dr Klaus was a local man, the son and grandson of farmers. He knew everyone and everything, and the word was that in an emergency, he would treat sick animals as well. He lived alone in a big house in W., following the death of his wife. He said if Michael promised to keep God out of it, he was welcome and might come. He was an atheist, said the doctor, no, not even an atheist, he believed in nothing, not even that there was no God. He was a man of science, not faith. A Communist, thought Michael, and he said, All right, all right, and suppressed a yawn.

The doctor served schnapps, and because Michael had a question, he drank the schnapps, drank it in one swallow, and then another glass that Dr Klaus poured him. Mandy, said Michael, whether ... and ... He was sweating. She claimed her baby wasn't the outcome of union with a man, that she had never, no, that no man had known ... My God: you know what I'm trying to say. The doctor emptied his glass and asked whether Michael meant the Lord had a hand in the business, or maybe a peter. Michael stared at him with an empty, despairing expression. He drank the schnapps the doctor had poured him, and stood up. The hymen, he said quietly, almost inaudibly, the hymen. That would be a miracle, said the doctor, and here in our midst. He laughed. Michael excused himself. I am a man of science, said the doctor, you are a man of faith. Let's not mix things up. I know what I know; you believe whatever you like.

On his way back, Michael was sweating still more profusely. He grew dizzy. Blood pressure, he thought. He sat down on the grassy edge of a large beet field. The beets had already been harvested and were lying in long heaps along the road. In the distance he could see a strip of woodland, and in the middle of the enormous field was the little island that his housekeeper had spoken of, a few trees sprouting from the dark earth.

Michael stood up and took a step into the field, and then another one. He walked toward the island. The damp soil clung to his boots in great clumps, and he stumbled, reeled, walking was difficult. Be of good heart, he thought, howbeit we must be cast upon a certain island. He walked on.

Once he heard a car drive past on the road. He didn't look around. He crossed the field, step by step, and finally the trees came nearer and he was there, and it really was like an island: the furrows of ploughed land had divided and opened, as if an island had erupted from the land, and torn the soil aside like a curtain. This island was maybe half a yard in elevation. At its edge grew some grass, beyond was shrubbery. Michael broke a twig off one of the bushes and scraped some of the earth off his soles. Then he walked around the island on the narrow strip of grass. In one place there was a gap in the vegetation, and he climbed through it and got to a small clearing under the trees. The tall grass was trampled down, and there were a couple of empty bottles.

Michael looked up: between the tops of the trees he could see the sky, it seemed not so high as over the field. It was very quiet. The air was warm, even though the sun was far gone to the west. Michael took off his jacket and dropped it on the grass. Then, without really knowing what he was doing, he unbuttoned his shirt and took it off, and then his undershirt, his shoes, his pants, his shorts, and last of all his socks. He took off his wristwatch and dropped it on the pile of clothes, and then his glasses and the ring his mother had given him for protection. And stood there the way God had made him: as naked as a sign.

Michael looked up at the sky. He had never felt more connected to it. He lifted his arms aloft, then he felt the dizziness of a moment before, and he toppled forward onto his knees, and knelt there, naked with upraised arms. He began singing, softly and with a cracked voice, but it wasn't enough. And so he screamed, screamed as loudly as he could, because he knew that out here only God could hear him, and that God heard him and was looking down at him.

¶ As he walked back home across the field, he thought about Mandy, and she was very near to him, as though she was in him. So he thought, without knowing it, I have given shelter to an angel.

Back in the vicarage, Michael went straight to the old sideboard, and got out a bottle of schnapps that a farmer had given him after the burial of his wife, and poured himself a little glassful and then a second. Then he lay down, and only woke when the housekeeper called him down to supper. He had a headache.

And what if it's true? he said as the housekeeper brought in supper. What if what's true? Mandy. If she's conceived. By whom? Is not this land also a desert? said Michael. How do we know that He doesn't direct His gaze here, and that this child has found favour in His eyes, this Mandy? The housekeeper shook her head angrily: Her father's a bus driver. Well wasn't Joseph a carpenter? But that was a long time

F

ago. Didn't she believe that God was still alive and in our midst? And that Jesus will return? Sure. But not here. What's special about Mandy? She's nothing. She works in the restaurant in W., she helps out.

With God nothing shall be impossible, said Michael, and verily, I say unto you, that the publicans and the harlots go into the kingdom of God before you. The housekeeper made a face and disappeared into the kitchen. Michael had never managed to persuade her to eat with him: she had always said she didn't want there to be talk in the village. Talk about what? We're only human, she said then, we all have our needs.

❡ After supper Michael went out again. He walked down the street, and the dogs in the yards barked like crazy, and Michael thought, You would do better to trust in God than in your dogs. That was the Communists' doing: he should have talked them around, but he hadn't done it. There were no more people in the church now than in the spring, and you could hear of immorality and drunkenness every day.

Michael went into the retirement home and asked for Frau Schmidt, who read the lesson every week. If she's still awake, said Ulla, the nurse, unwillingly, and disappeared. A Communist, thought Michael, bound to be. He could tell, he knew what they thought when they saw him. And then, when someone passed away, they called him anyway. So that he gets a decent funeral, Ulla had said once, when he was required to bury a man who hadn't been inside a church in his life.

Frau Schmidt was still awake. She was sitting in her comfy chair watching WHO WANTS TO BE A MILLIONAIRE. Michael shook her hand, Good evening, Frau Schmidt. He pulled up a chair and sat down beside her. She had read nicely, he said, and he wanted to thank her for it again. Frau Schmidt nodded from the waist. Michael took a small leather–bound Bible from his pocket. Today I'd like to read you something, he said. And while the TV quiz host asked which city was destroyed by a volcanic eruption in 79 A.D., Troy, Sodom, Pompeii, or Babylon, Michael read aloud, and steadily more loudly. There shall come in the last days scoffers, walking after their own lusts, and saying, Where is the promise of his coming? for since the fathers fell asleep, all things continue as from the beginning of the creation. But, beloved, be not ignorant of this one thing, that one day with the Lord is as a thousand years, and a thousand years as one day.

And he read, the day of the Lord will come as a thief in the night; in which the heavens shall pass away with a great noise, and the elements shall melt with fervent heat, and the earth also and the works that are therein shall be burned up.

All the while Michael read, the old woman nodded: she rocked back and forth, as if her whole body were one great yes. Then finally she spoke, and said, It's not Sodom, and it's not Babylon. Is it Troy?

The day is perhaps closer than we imagine, said Michael. But no one will know.

I don't know, said Frau Schmidt. He will come like a thief in the night, said Michael, standing up. Troy, said Frau Schmidt. He shook her hand. She didn't say anything, and didn't look when he left the room. Pompeii, said the quiz host. Pompeii, said Frau Schmidt.

No one will know it, thought Michael as he went home. The dogs of the Communists were barking, and once he bent down to pick up a stone and hurled it against a wooden gate. That made the dog behind bark still more loudly, and Michael hurried on, so that no one would spot him. He didn't go back to the rectory, though, he walked out of the village.

It was half an hour to W. A single car passed him. He saw the beam of the headlights a long way ahead, and hid behind one of the trees lining the road until it was safely past. The island was nothing but a dark stain in the gray field, and it seemed to be closer than during the day. The stars were glittering: it had turned cold.

There was no one on the streets in W. The lights were on in the houses, and there was a single streetlamp at a crossroads. Michael knew where Mandy lived. He stopped at the garden gate and looked at the small singlestory house. He saw shadows moving in the kitchen. It looked like someone was doing the dishes. Michael felt his heart grow warmer. He leaned against the gate. Then he heard breathing very close by, and suddenly a loud, yelping bark. He jumped back and ran off. He wasn't a hundred yards away when the door of the house opened, and the beam of a flashlight showed in the darkness, and a man's voice shouted, Shut yer noise!

¶ On one of the following days, Michael went to the restaurant in W., where his housekeeper had said Mandy was helping out. And so it proved.

The dining room was high ceilinged. The walls were yellowed with cigarette smoke, the windows were blind, the furniture aged, and nothing went with anything else. There was no one there but Mandy, standing behind the bar as if she belonged there, with her hands on the counter. She smiled and lowered her gaze, and Michael had the sense of her face glowing in the gloomy room. He sat down at a table near the entrance. Mandy went over to him, he ordered tea, she disappeared. Please no one come, he thought to himself. Then Mandy came back with his tea. Michael added sugar and stirred. Mandy was still standing beside the table. An angel at my side, thought Michael. He took a hurried sip and burned his mouth. And then, not looking at Mandy, nor she looking at him, he spoke.

But of that day and hour knoweth no man, no, not the angels of heaven, but my Father only. But as the days of Noah were, so shall also the coming of the Son of man be. For as in the days that were before the flood they were eating and drinking, marrying and giving in marriage, until the flood came, and took them all away; so shall also the coming of the Son of man be.

F

Only now did Michael look at Mandy, and he saw that she was crying. Fear not, he said. Then he stood up and laid his hand on Mandy's head, and then he hesitated, and placed his other hand on her belly. Will it be called Jesus? Mandy asked softly. Michael was taken aback. He hadn't considered that. The wind bloweth where it listeth, he said, and thou hearest the sound thereof, but canst not tell whence it cometh, and whither it goeth.

Then he gave Mandy the little manual for young women and expectant mothers that the church provides, and from which he drew all his understanding, and he said Mandy should come to instruction, and to service, that was the most important thing, she had plenty to catch up on.

¶ Months passed. Autumn gave way to winter, the first snows fell and covered everything, the villages, the forest, and the fields. Winter stretched out over the land, and the acrid smell of woodsmoke hung heavy over the streets.

Michael went on long walks over the countryside, he went from village to village, and he went again across the large sugar-beet field, that was now frozen, to the island. Once again he stood there and raised his arms aloft. But the trees had lost their leaves, and the sky was distant. Michael waited for a sign. None came: there was no new star in the sky, no angel on the field to talk to him, no king and no shepherd and no sheep. Then he felt ashamed and thought, I am not chosen. She, Mandy, will receive the signal, it is to her the angel will appear.

Mandy was now coming in from W. on her moped every Wednesday to class, and every Sunday to church. Her belly was growing, but her face was growing thinner and pale. After service she stayed behind in church until everyone was gone, and then she sat with Michael in one of the pews, speaking quietly. Her baby was due in February, she said. If only it had been Christmas, thought Michael, if only it had been Easter. But Christmas was soon, while Easter was the end of March: they would see.

Then the housekeeper put her head through the door, and asked if the minister proposed to eat his lunch today. All the trouble she went to, she said, and not a word of praise, nothing, and then he left half of it. Michael said Mandy should stay for lunch, there was enough for two. For three, he added, and both smiled shyly. Why don't we just open a restaurant, said the housekeeper, laying a second setting. She banged the plates down on the table and stalked off without a word, and certainly without wishing them *Bon appétit*.

Mandy said her father was tormenting her, he insisted on knowing who the father was, and he went into a rage when she said it was Almighty God. No, he didn't beat her. Only slaps, she said, her mother as well. She wanted to leave home. They both ate in silence. Michael very little, Mandy twice helping herself to more. Do you like it? he asked. She nodded and blushed. Then he said, why didn't she live here in the rectory, there was room enough. Mandy looked at him timidly.

You can't do that, said the housekeeper. Michael said nothing. If you do that, I'm out of here, said the housekeeper. Still Michael said nothing. He crossed his arms. He thought of Bethlehem. Not this time, he thought. And the thought gave him strength. I'm moving out, said the housekeeper, and Michael nodded slowly. So much the better, he thought: he had already concluded that this housekeeper had been a Communist, and who knows what besides. Because she always said she was only human, and because her name was Carola, which was a heathen name. He had heard the stories about her and his predecessor, a married man. In the sacristy, they said, among other things. That woman had nothing to say to him. She least of all. And she wasn't even a good cook.

The housekeeper disappeared into the kitchen, and then she left the house, because it wasn't right and it wasn't proper. And Mandy moved in: she was the new housekeeper, that was the agreement worked out with her parents. She was even paid. But Mandy was already in her fifth month, and her belly was so big that she snorted like a cow when she went up the stairs, and Michael was afraid something might happen to the baby one day when she lugged the heavy carpets out to beat them.

Michael was just returning from one of his walks when he saw Mandy beating the carpets in front of the vicarage. He said she ought to take it easy, and carried the carpets back into the house himself, even if it was almost more than he could do: his body wasn't very strong. Everything has to be clean by Christmas, said Mandy. That pleased Michael, and seemed to him to be a good sign. Other than that he hadn't found much evidence of faith, even if she liked to swear Holy Mother of God, and was firmly convinced that her baby was a baby Jesus, as she put it. She did say she was Protestant. But not so very much. Michael was in doubt. He felt ashamed of his doubts, but there they were, poisoning his love and his belief.

From now on, Michael did all the housework himself. Mandy cooked for him, and they ate together in the dark dining room, without speaking much. Michael worked far into the evenings. He read his Bible, and when he heard Mandy come out of the bathroom, he waited for five minutes, he was no longer able to work, that's how excited he was. Then he knocked on the door of Mandy's room, and she called, Come in, come in. There she was, already in bed, with her hand on her brow, or else on the blanket, over her belly.

On one occasion he asked her about her dreams: after all, he was waiting for a sign. But Mandy didn't dream. She slept deeply and solidly, she said. So he asked her if she really hadn't ever had a boyfriend or anything, and if she'd ever found blood on her sheets. Not during your period, he said, and he felt very peculiar, talking to her like that. If she is the new mother of God, then what sort of figure will I cut, he

F

thought. Mandy didn't reply. She cried, and said, didn't he believe her? He laid his hand on the blanket and his eyes got moist. We should be called the children of God, he said, therefore the world knoweth us not, because it knew Him not. What Him? asked Mandy.

Once she pushed the blankets back and lay before him in her thin nightie. Michael had had his hand on the blanket, and then he raised it up, and now it was hovering in the air over Mandy's belly. It's moving, said Mandy, and she took his hand with both of hers and pulled it down so that it pressed against her belly, and Michael couldn't raise his hand, it lay there for a long time, heavy and sinful.

•

Christmas came and went. On Christmas Eve, Mandy went to her parents, but the next day she was back again. There were not many people in church. In the village there was talk about Michael and Mandy, letters had been written to the bishop, and letters were written back from the bishop. A call had gone out, and a representative of the bishop had traveled to the village on a Sunday, and had sat with Michael and spoken with him. On that day, Mandy had eaten in the kitchen. She was very excited, but when the visitor left, Michael said everything was fine: the bishop knew there was a lot of bad blood in the district, and that some old Communists were still fighting against the church, and sowing division.

With the passing of time, the baby grew, and Mandy's belly got ever bigger, long after Michael thought it couldn't possibly. As if it wasn't part of her body. And so Michael laid his hand on the growing baby, and felt happiness.

The terrible thing happened when Michael went off on one of his afternoon walks. He realised he had left his book at home. He turned back, and half an hour later had returned. He quietly let himself into the house and tiptoed up the stairs. Mandy often slept in the daytime now, and if that was the case now, he didn't want to wake her. But when he stepped into his room, Mandy was standing there naked: she was standing in front of the large mirror in the door of the wardrobe. And she was looking at herself from the side, and so confronted Michael, who could see everything. Mandy had heard him coming and had turned to face him, and they looked at each other, just exactly as they were.

What are you doing in my room? asked Michael. And he hoped Mandy would cover her nakedness with her hands, but she did not. Her hands hung at her sides like the leaves of a tree, barely stirring. She said she had no mirror in her room, and she had wanted to see this belly she had grown. Michael approached Mandy, so as not to have to look at her anymore. Then his hands touched her hands, and then he thought about nothing at all, because he was with Mandy, and she was with him. And so it was that Michael's hand lay there, as if it had been newly brought forth: an animal from out of that wound.

Then Michael did sleep, and when he awakened, he thought, my God, what have I done. He lay there curled in bed, and with his hand covered his sin, which was great. Mandy's blood was her witness and his proof, and he was surprised that the elements did not melt with fervent heat, or the heavens pass away with a great noise: to slay him and punish him with lightning or some other event. But this did not transpire.

•

Nor did the heavens open when Michael hurried along the street on the way to W. He was on his way to the island in the field, and he walked rapidly and with stumbling steps across the frozen furrows. Mandy had been asleep when he left the house, Mandy, whom he had taken in and to whom he had offered the hospitality of his house.

He reached the island and sat down in the snow. He could not stand any longer, so tired was he and so sad and lost. He would stay there and never leave. Let them find him, the farmer and the woman when they came here in spring to commit adultery.

It was cold and getting dark. Then it was night. Michael was still sitting on his island in the snow. The damp soaked through his coat, and he shivered and felt chilled to the bone. Let us not love one another with words, he thought, nor with speech. But with deeds. So God had led him to Mandy, and Mandy to him: that they might love one another. For she was not a child, she was eighteen or nineteen. And was it not written that no one should know? Was it not written that the day would come like a thief? So Michael thought: I cannot know. And if it was God's will that she conceive His child, then it was also His will that she had received him: for was he not God's work and creature?

Through the trees Michael could see only a few scattered stars. But when he left their cover and stepped out onto the field, he saw all the stars that can be seen on a cold night, and for the first time since he had come here, he was not afraid of this sky. And he was glad that the sky was so distant, and that he himself was so small on this endless field. So distant that even God had to take a second look to see him.

Soon he was back in the village. The dogs barked, and Michael threw stones at the gates and barked himself, and aped the dogs, their stupid yapping and howling, and he laughed when the dogs were beside themselves with rage and fury: and he was beside himself just as much.

In the vicarage the lights were on, and as soon as Michael stepped inside, he could smell the dinner that Mandy had cooked. And as he took off his sodden boots and his heavy coat, she stepped out into the kitchen doorway and looked anxiously at him. It

F

had gotten cold, he said, and she said dinner was ready. Then Michael stepped up to Mandy, and he kissed her on the mouth, as she smiled up at him. Over supper they discussed one possible name for the baby, and then another one. And when it was bedtime they squeezed each other's hands, and each went to their own room.

As it got colder and colder in January, and it was almost impossible to heat the old vicarage, Mandy moved one evening from the guest bedroom into the warmer room of the master of the house. She carried her blanket in front of her, and lay down beside Michael as he moved aside, without a word. And that night, and in all the nights to come, they lay in one bed, and so learned to know and to love one another better. And Michael saw everything, and Mandy was not ashamed.

But was it a sin? Who could know. And hadn't Mandy's own blood affirmed that it was a child of God that was growing, a child of purity? Could there be anything impure about purity?

Even if Michael hadn't thought it possible, his word reached the people and the Communists of the village. They were touched by the wonder that had occurred, and one couldn't say how: for such people came to the door and knocked. They came without many words, and brought what they had. A neighbour brought a cake. She had been baking, she said, and it was no more trouble to bake two than one. And was Mandy doing all right?

On another day, Marco the publican came around and asked how far along they were. Michael invited him in, and called Mandy, and made tea in the kitchen. Then the three of them sat at the table and were silent, because they didn't know what to say. Marco had brought along a bottle of cognac, and set it down in front of them. He knew full well, he said, that it wasn't the right thing for a small baby, but maybe if it had a colic. Then he asked to have it explained to him, and when Michael did so, Marco looked at Mandy and her belly with disbelief. Was that certain? he asked, and Michael said no one knew, and no one could know. Because it was pretty unlikely, Marco said. He had picked up the cognac again, and was looking at the bottle. He seemed to hesitate, but then he put it back on the table, and said, three stars, that's the best you can get hereabouts. Not the one I serve my customers. And he was a little confused, and he stood up and scratched his head. Back in the summer you rode pillion on my bike, he said, and he laughed, think of it. They'd gone bathing, the whole lot of them, in the lake outside F. Who'd have thought it.

When Marco left, Frau Schmidt was standing in the garden, with something she had knitted for the baby. With her was Nurse Ulla from the retirement home, whom Michael had suspected of being a Communist. But she was bringing something herself, a soft toy, and she wanted Mandy to touch her as well.

It was one after another. The table in the front room was covered with presents, and the cupboard housed a dozen or more bottles of schnapps. The children brought drawings of Mandy and the baby, and sometimes Michael was in the pictures too, and perhaps an ass or an ox as well.

Before long the people were coming from W. and the other villages, wanting to see the expectant mother, to ask her advice on this or that matter. And Mandy gave them advice and comfort, and sometimes she would lay her hand on the arm or the head of the people, without saying anything. She had become so earnest and still that even Michael seemed to see her anew. And did all that needed to be done. In the village, various quarrels were settled during these days, and even the dogs seemed to be less ferocious when Michael walked down the street, and on some houses the straw stars and Christmas wreaths were back up on the doors again, and in the windows, because the whole village was rejoicing, as though Christmas was yet to come. Everyone knew it, but no one said it.

One time, Dr Klaus came to see that all was well. But when he knocked on the door, Michael did not welcome him in. He sat upstairs with Mandy, and they were quiet as two children, and peeked out of the window until they saw the doctor leaving.

The next day, Michael went to W. to see the doctor. He poured schnapps, and asked how things stood with Mandy. Michael didn't touch the schnapps. He merely said everything was fine, and they didn't need a doctor. And these stories that were making the rounds? He that is of the earth is earthly, and speaketh of the earth, said Michael. Be that as it may, said the doctor, the baby will be born on earth, and not in heaven. And if you need help, then call me, and I'll come. Then they shook hands, and nothing more was said. Michael, though, went back to the retirement home in the village and spoke to Nurse Ulla. She had four children herself, and knew the ropes. And she promised him she would assist when the time came.

Then in February, the time came: the baby was born. Mandy was assisted by Michael, and by Nurse Ulla, whom he had called in. As word spread of the impending event, people gathered on the village streets to wait in silence. It was already dark when the baby was born, and Ulla stepped up to the window and held it aloft, that all might see it. And it was a girl.

Michael sat at Mandy's bedside, holding her hand and looking at the baby. She's no beauty, said Mandy, but that was more of a question. And Nurse Ulla asked the new mother where she meant to go with her baby, as she would no longer be able to run the minister's household anymore. Then Michael said: He that hath the bride is the bridegroom. And he kissed Mandy in full view of the nurse. And she later told everyone of it: that he had given his word.

Because the child could not be called Jesus, they called it Sandra. And as the people in the village believed it had been born for them, they didn't mind that it was a girl. And all were contented and rejoiced.

The following Sunday attendance at church was greater than it had been for a long time. Mandy and the babe sat in the front pew. The organ was playing, and after it had played, Michael climbed up to the pulpit and spoke as follows: Whether this is a child that has long been awaited in the world, we do not know, and may not know. For you yourselves know perfectly that the day of the Lord so cometh as a thief in the night. But ye, brethren, are not in darkness. For they that sleep sleep in the night; and they that be drunken are drunken in the night. But let us, who are of the day, be sober.

That which is born of the flesh is flesh, said Michael, and that which is born of the Spirit is spirit. But we, beloved, should be called the children of God.

INTERVIEW

WITH

KESTON SUTHERLAND

SAID BY THE *NEW STATESMAN* to be 'at the forefront of the experimental movement in contemporary British poetry', Keston Sutherland's poetic and critical work is a headrush. High on its own sensitivity, his writings explode the familiar modes of poetry, fusing the lyric tradition with the high-octane languages of protest, stock market exchange and information technology, with the individuated vocabularies of biochemistry, geology and neurology. A sardonic yet rhapsodic disdain for high-capitalist consumerism and yappy Fox News neo-conservatism has won him international acclaim, and has given rise to six collections of poetry, numerous essays on poetics, politics and philosophy, his critical journal *QUID* and the co-founding of 'nonconformist poetry' publisher Barque Press.

We met on a steely day in Sutherland's hometown, Brighton, where he is Reader in English at the University of Sussex. What follows is an edited version of a spooling conversation, ranging from 'Enron to Xbox' and back again, occasioned by the upcoming publication of his newest collection *THE ODES TO TL61P* (Enitharmon Press, April 2013). A poetry of unworkable postures and melodic germination, made famous by his astonishingly energetic readings (now widely available on Youtube), Sutherland rose to international eminence with the publication of a special edition of the *CHICAGO REVIEW* in 2007, positioning his work alongside that of Andrea Brady, Chris Goode, Simon Jarvis and Peter Manson, and forming a major reconsideration of the field of contemporary poetry in Britain today. Studying under Jeremy Prynne during his years at Cambridge, he is nevertheless resistant to the coterie demands of the 'Cambridge School', preferring instead to enter into critical dialogues with the visual arts, improvised music, and multilingual texts.

Typified by a rampant lyricism, the warped soundbites and shifting logics of his work nevertheless confront political and social events; his collection *STRESS POSITION* enacts torture sequences observed in Abu Ghraib and Guantanamo Bay, and the demented puppetry of *HOT WHITE ANDY*, hailed by John Wilkinson as 'the most remarkable poem published in English this century', rages against our attitudes to twenty-first century consumerism. His newest collection comments on all the 'mucky adult clay' that comprises our pressed political landscape and yet marks a distinct shift in tone and composition. Characterised by Sutherland as 'a kind of album or masque of metrical variations, everything from strictly perfected tetrameters to the most psychotic arrhythmia', *THE ODES TO TL61P* upends the conventions of prose poetry. At once a eulogy to a now departed object – *TL61P* is the code for a replacement part of a now defunct Hotpoint washer-dryer – it is also a deeply felt meditation on all that is inexplicable.

———

^Q THE WHITE REVIEW — The poet and critic John Wilkinson argues that a 'lyric turn' has taken place in experimental British poetry over the last decade, characterised by a 'politically engaged writing of multiple ambiguity, corrosive agents and a horizon of indescribable plenitude with the felt necessity to light a path towards an identifiable and attainable political objective'. Would you agree? Is this 'felt necessity', however various the 'political objectives', the unifying pressure in contemporary British poetry?

^A KESTON SUTHERLAND — It is difficult for me to guess at this moment where a common and spacious enough ground could be found for the poets that I know to stand together hand in hand and put their names to a collective document, such as some kind of manifesto. I think there is a stroppy and robust individualism of a fairly healthy kind among many British poets, which has caused a sometimes hypersensitive attitude of suspicion towards collective utterance and collective decision-taking. Many years ago I believed passionately that poets who hoped to have any political agency ought to get together and decide on principles and terms and aims. I sometimes still do. More practically, I wanted to create a culture of free exchange of works, and of interventions into public life, which would fashion an altogether different kind of political poetry.

One of the difficulties is that the more passionately poets think about social problems, and about capital and about government and about wars and about the politics of sexuality, the more they, the best of them at least, tend to drill down into profoundly idiosyncratic attitudes and positions. I say idiosyncratic rather than individualist. That's been my experience. Part of the intrinsic pressure of being a poet is the flight from generality and into the aggressively and irreconcilably, absolutely singular. It's very difficult to feel continually torn in two different directions, to feel that surge into the singular, which is a deeply private pressure that comes from childhood and from love and from sex and from any coagulation of other ends and places, and then on the other hand to want to work, to build, to assert a collective political project and political identity. I think that pressure, which can and perhaps ought to threaten to tear poets apart, must be lived and learned from, rather than simply denied in the name of an automatic and unanswerable collectivism.

It is also true that there is a great level of disagreement at the level of principle between poets. The American L=A=N=G=U=A=G=E poets decided, perhaps admirably, that they had enough of an interest in fashioning a manifesto, that they could explore their differences collectively, under a common title, in collectively-built venues, publications and environments. That hasn't happened with the same public coherence in Britain. I am nonetheless very excited by John's eloquent description; a discovery of new energies, and felt political objectives, felt political necessities, in British poetry of the moment. I especially like that he specifies that these pressures are 'felt', and not merely argued into, or imagined or speculated.

For me, the pressure which sustains poetry as a lyrical art, and which still compels me to write, is something very akin to what Marx described as the 'absolutely imperative need for revolution'. For Marx, that was a specifically and exclusively proletarian experience. Perhaps that's right, perhaps historically Marx was attempting then to define an experience and a physiology of need which only the proletariat can authentically express. It remains, nonetheless, the horizon of my poetry to attempt to express with the maximum conceivable and liveable pressure an absolutely imperative need for the comprehensive revolutionary transformation of human experience and relations.

Q. THE WHITE REVIEW — Did this 'need' give rise to Barque Press, the publishing house you run with fellow founder Andrea Brady?

A. KESTON SUTHERLAND — No, not really. We started Barque Press because we were flirting with each other... We were both fledgling poets at the time, and part of the way we were growing into that was by hanging out late at night and reading our poems to each other. We thought it was probably quite unlikely that anyone else would want to publish us, so one day we decided to get a stapler and some photocopier paper and just do it ourselves. It was a very exciting moment in Cambridge, and I remember feeling intoxicated, surrounded by so many dizzyingly difficult and formidable poets. I wanted nothing more than to levitate into their ranks. I thought that by starting this, I was joining a culture of gift exchange, a culture of militant samizdat exclusion from the circuits of mainstream publication. And so we were. I wanted to publish as many other people's work as I could, to extend these gifts as far and as wide as I could, to encourage young writers like myself to believe in the value of small editions and work that had no pre-existing audience or apparatus of promotion, books whose status as commodities was very marginal and tenuous. That was a culture of production with a very exciting and worthwhile politics, and I still believe in that.

However, I've increasingly grown to feel that, for my own work at least, I don't want to inhabit only that one context of the circulation of gifts. There's a passage in Marx's EIGHTEENTH BRUMAIRE OF LOUIS NAPOLEON where he says that the shipwreck of the June insurrection by the proletariat was a consequence of their attempt to revolutionise society behind society's back. Now I don't mean to propose a grandiose comparison, but it does strike me that a too inward-looking culture of poetry publication and circulation, sometimes without altogether reflecting on its own potential audiences and its relations to the world, can have the same slightly fantastical ambition to create a revolution in culture behind society's back. Which it also hopes will be a revolution in politics behind society's back.

The best poetry in the UK has for the last sixty years come out of that context, and continues to. But I've wanted for a while now to risk venturing out into a potentially uncomprehending or even hostile public space, quite without imperious or supercilious designs on anybody's intelligence, without thinking that I am a standard bearer for more advanced tendencies, and to reach out to people who may have no sense of what to make of this work, and to learn from them myself.

Any serious socialist politics has to think in that way, and in that way has to be prepared to absorb, learn from and accommodate forms of presently ambivalent or difficult relations with other parts of culture and other parts of society. Depending on what the work of mine may be, I may decide to position it somewhere relatively obscure, and in that way to keep alive certain possibilities of gift exchange that matter to me. Or, as with THE ODES TO TL61P, I might decide to place it in the widest circulation that any work of mine may be able to achieve, to speak to people that I don't know, to speak to strangers, without any preconceptions of what this may do to them.

Q. THE WHITE REVIEW — In spite of the provisional and shifting nature of your work, you do also reference real political and social events – I'm thinking of your collection STRESS POSITION which enacts torture sequences observed in Abu Ghraib and Guantanamo Bay, or your poem '10/11/10' (sitting within the body of THE ODES) on the student protests at Millbank. All of your 'mucky adult clay' is rammed into that poem...

A. KESTON SUTHERLAND — Yes, ha, the 'mucky adult clay', which you are pressed into, or so the poem tells you in a hectoring tone which I hope people may find ungratefully grating. 'Clay' is interesting as the substance used to describe the very origins of humanity, that man was formed from the clay in which God moulded him, so that we were all made out of this originally pliable substance. Clay has always been a substance of the origin, best mashed up into an allotrope of dust, the substance of extinction; this poem derails and perverts that myth of substance. Here it's adulthood, rather than the origin, which is the clay; childhood is not clay in this poem, childhood is curiously something much harder and more fixed and definite, at points at least, than adulthood ever is.

There is also a pun here, 'pressed into a mucky adult clay': the clay is adulterated. Marx was very interested, in DAS KAPITAL, in the chapter on the working day, in the adulteration of substances, particularly of bread. In other words, the ruination of what ought to be useful substances by their infection or through the intrusion of alien substances, such as dust, grit, dirt. News of adulteration provokes in the bourgeois consumer a sudden frenzy of interest in the social history of production. Now that my meat has shit in it, I suddenly want to know who made it and how. Adulteration in that way provides a momentary and spectacular pretext for subduing commodity fetishism. The 'mucky adult clay' is a substance which ought by adulthood, if it really is the mythical origin of our originally malleable selfhood, to have set, to have taken shape, ought even to have been shaped into a useful vessel of some kind, something which can contain life. Instead it remains, in this poem, permanently mucky and maybe even gets progressively muckier: you become a more pliable, shifty, indefinite substance. A sloppier identity. 'Mucky', too, is a word that parents use to chastise their children, who are snapped at for being 'mucky'.

Q. THE WHITE REVIEW —— Is this a literature more polemical than poetic?

A. KESTON SUTHERLAND —— To some extent it is polemical. One of the liberties which I've consciously decided to take in this work has been to speak very directly about current events, about living individuals – both celebrities, figures in public life, and figures from my own life, my own history – and often, again consciously and with a kind of painful consciousness that I was doing something contrary to my own writerly instincts, I have often adopted an idiom which is violently and programmatically explicit. In that sense yes, it feels to me often polemical but, in what I hope is a richly complicated sense, as an ironical and sometimes obviously factitious style of polemic, which rests in turn on an intimate investigation of the meaning of, and possibilities for, making things explicit, for becoming explicit. That is pushed much further in this book than in any of my previous works. The explicitation in THE ODES is ramped up to almost deranged extremes, pushed right up against the inexplicable and into the infinitesimals of hurtful recollection and unmoderatable desire. It was perhaps the nearest thing to a principle of composition for me, as I was working, that I would try – as transgressively and confrontationally as I possibly could – to produce new powers of explicitation and of the explicit in this work. To own up to, to stare at, and to confront facts, possibilities, sensations, pleasures, disappointments in my life, and to do that as squarely and with as little real prevarication as I was capable of reducing myself to. That sometimes becomes polemical, or assumes a polemical surface aspect.

Q. THE WHITE REVIEW —— You are often taken to task for the difficult nature of your verse. The suggestion is that, due to its difficulty, it can only ever be for certain communities, or certain readerships; a coterie language or a closed realm of reference. How do you overcome that risk?

A. KESTON SUTHERLAND — First of all I would try to *understand* and acknowledge the objection, in whatever form the individual reader may wish to make it. I don't feel instinctively or irremediably sceptical about the resistances to my work or to this culture of poetry.

Q. THE WHITE REVIEW — The most virulent of which were probably brought to bear against the work of Jeremy Prynne...

A. KESTON SUTHERLAND — Yes, and there probably always will be attacks like that against Prynne. Prynne's work, which I love enormously and have learned from immeasurably, may never emerge suddenly into a clarity of full disclosure, like broadest magical daylight, and assume its place on the curriculum of canonical texts, laid open for everyone to enjoy absolutely equally and on equal terms. Of course, that's just as true of Shakespeare as it is of Prynne, it's just as true of what might seem apparently to be the simplest type of poem – such as William Blake's poetry, Frank O'Hara's poetry, poems which any reader might instantly, even if only at the level of sensation, at first sight be excited or moved by.

These poems, under the pressure of a long-lasting and thorough engagement, when they are really lived with, begin to metamorphose, they shift, they metastasise, they become different objects. I think that's just as true for poetry which is explicitly simple and congenial in its use of language, as it is for poetry that is truculent and obfuscatory with its use of language. The psychological, psychosexual, social and political dynamics and the mechanisms at play in reactions to difficulty are interesting to me. Lots of things in my life I find very difficult; many of them other people may not find difficult. Difficulty for me extends across a great variety of experiences and modes of existing in the world and means

of responding to things.

What I would say about my newer work, and also about some of my older poems, is that they are perhaps not so difficult to understand – if what we mean by that is the basic construal of their grammar, the ability to summarise some of their propositions, the ability to follow discursive constructions and lines of argument – as they are difficult to accept. For me, the difficulty of acceptance is much more radical, in this work at least. How do we accept that we will all die under a system of vampiric ruthless exploitation? What does it mean to live with that?

When I say that it's difficult to accept, I don't mean that I'm trying to find the terms on which I could accept it. I mean that at a fundamental level, getting up in the morning, going on living, paying taxes and working in the world, being a wage labourer, requires – at least in outward behaviour and practice – expressions of acceptance, which can be formidably difficult to live with. I'm trying in my poetry to investigate the profoundest difficulties of acceptance that I can find.

Now, it may be that some readers would disagree with me, would claim that whether it's acceptable or not, it's still very difficult to understand – and I can understand why someone might say that. It could be that they expect a poem to deliver certain sorts of satisfaction or gratification, and they will think that my poetry is too demented and too heterogeneous and too crazy, really, to deliver what they expect from a poem. It might be that the quantity of material packed into the poem is so gigantic that they feel overloaded, or disoriented by it, perhaps even dizzy. Or it might be that it's so consistently hyperallusive, and seems to make reference to so many contexts, names, other authorships, that they nervously imagine that without the knowledge of all of these various connections, they are not the intended or proper readers of these poems. As if there was such a thing!

I've been conscious of all of those potential discomforts or dissatisfactions that readers might experience, but I've nonetheless worked on *THE ODES* long enough, and I hope generously and carefully enough, that I've tried to write something which will make all of those forms of discomfort and difficulty productive for people. So I've not tried to reassure readers in advance, but I have tried honestly to extend the possibility of a new relation of comprehension between individuals. This might require some work, might require some daring, might require a trying longevity of relation.

Q. THE WHITE REVIEW — We've been speaking about lyric and polemic in your writing, and the necessary fudging of the two. Would you say that it is possible to be both a poet *and* a political being? Or are they two distinct personhoods?

A. KESTON SUTHERLAND — I think politics has a number of distinct identities or meanings. There are a number of overlapping but not perfectly co-extensive fields of operation that we would call 'political'. In one sense politics is nothing more than what professional politicians do. If we define politics narrowly like that, we get an emphatic account of the value of the social, that what really matters is social relations – what really matters is us, who are not politicians, and how in spite of and at war with politics, we can rebuild and redesign our own ways of relating to each other, against those formal institutions. In that sense I would say that I am a political being only because of a deeply resented conscription into a field of activity which fundamentally ought not to require political institutions of the present order. That is not to discount being a

political being, but to painfully accept it. But it is also to assert its provisionality.

Marx often distinguished between politics and socialism, stating that socialism starts where politics ends. In another, broader sense, politics might extend to just about anything we do, think or feel. I feel that when I'm writing poetry my mind, my senses, and my body are all in unpredictable ways politically active. At times this is perfectly explicit in my poems, as in the section of 'Ode 5' subtitled '10/11/10', about the student protests in London. That is absolutely direct political poetry. What is crucial to me is that it is direct, that it is completely undisguised, that it is aggressively emphatic, and that is a socialist and realist art which attempts to describe the real detail of social relations and to find the intrinsic forms of contradiction which structure social relations, one of the fundamental forms of which is the permanent and ongoing contradiction under capital between the means of production and the relations of production. My poetry is always in some sense about precisely that: what is the material that we work or live with, what are the techniques for building and living with it, and, on the other hand, what are our relations between each other and what are the conscious and unconscious forms of mastery, of control, of manipulation, of affection, of togetherness and care which comprise the extent of our lives together – you might say a dialectic between technique and life. So I feel all the time, when I'm writing, thoroughly and consciously engaged with questions that at least have a political dimension and which extend to everything from 'Enron to Xbox'. Or further. The orgasm to Michael Gove.

At the same time, it is crucial to my conception of the present limits of poetic eloquence that there really is a significant material difference between writing poetry and being a politically effective agent in the world whose activity directly and unarguably transforms social relations, particularly if we mean transformation by collective or institutional means. Poetry with a restricted and small circulation whose specific temporality of self-disclosure can be very extended, and which might not make sense for a few decades to come, can hardly seem like the most effective form of direct political intervention. That for me is a problem, but it is also a fact that can be endlessly explored and reflected on from an infinite variety of angles. I try to do that with *THE ODES*, to explore the limits not only of agency but of inertia and of impotence. The danger is that reflection on impotence can easily degenerate into mannerism; but that risk too is socially meaningful and ought to be reflected on and tested.

It remains, nonetheless, a fundamental ambition of mine that my poetry will exercise some influence of a political character over living individuals, now, in this world, and that it will contribute meaningfully to creating, sustaining and enriching a vibrant communist public culture, in which it is a loyal and constant ambition to break down the forms of social paralysis and injustice, as well as of self-interested mastery and of exploitation, which under capital adulterate all of our relations with each other, even the most intimate. I want to turn those relations inside out and aggressively, beautifully, passionately and frantically find the most copious account I can make of how we can live together in a more profoundly generous way.

^{Q.} THE WHITE REVIEW — One critic noted that you represent 'what the future of British verse should look like'. What do you think the future of British verse could look like?

^{A.} KESTON SUTHERLAND — I deeply hope that

I don't know. I want it to be inconceivably astonishing to me. I want to encounter it as the most threatening and primitive freshness, I want to be so comprehensively confused by it that it takes me forever to learn to live with it and to reconcile the world that I already know with whatever this poetry is and does... I suppose, to be honest, that is my ambition as a writer for the future of my own poetry. I hope that the future of verse in this country, and everywhere, will be a future of more and more resolute, more passionately principled and more ardently dedicated confrontations with the injustices and machinery of capital, and that its interrogation of the structures of capital in living experience will be conducted more and more thoroughly, vibrantly and vitally. But I suspect that what will continue to happen, for a long time at least, is that lots of anxious and conservatively rather than radically narcissistic poets will go on writing verse which, with more or less justification, is meant to encapsulate and preserve in the aspic of sentimental memory and sensation the trivia of working-week-life and their surface profundities, poems that may only distantly touch upon the complexity of social relations, and then with a defensive, pretty archness. Or the audience will go on uncritically accepting that poetry is and ought to be in this way a modest and circumscribed art and, in its end, a comfortingly politically inert and ineffective one, from which the best we can hope for is lukewarm consolation.

I hope not. I hope not. I hope that, in Britain and everywhere else, amongst people who care about poetry, we might be persuaded, sooner or later, that there is no part, or detail, or potential of experience which cannot be radically addressed and transformed through the sheer delirious and euphoric momentum of powerfully expressive verse. I hope that might eventually become a collective ambition for readers and poets alike: to radically reconceive and feel again human relations in honour of and in the brilliant light of the power of poetry. The fundamental transformation of human life, that's what I hope for.

NATALIE FERRIS, JANUARY 2013

POEMS

BY

OLI HAZZARD
JOE LUNA
KESTON SUTHERLAND

FROM 'ECLOGUES'

24.

We read too much | into the ground | beneath | the ground beneath
our feet. Since everything that happened | happened there | it
bombed. Who knows what | Power failed along the lines. But like
Christopher Newman (a character | in Henry James's THE AMERICAN) I
prefer the copies | of masterpieces | over the originals. As Paul Nash
implied | perhaps to distinguish the trees | from the wood, its bark
is worse than | as Lee Harwood might say | all you do, my | is
appropriate. You mine | my mine | with yours. Steel yourself | for an
act of originality

                                                                    bite

that feeds it. The divisions | undivided | all the sweeter. I was
intimated across the threshold | of a margin | of a centre | moved by
the accents of a margin | a kind of latent relief. | Something | both
doubtable and redoubtable | a reliquary of limits. You could | snooze
by the light | of such names | and this is no | library, chief. Beware
po-faced Þōden for he knows | not what you do: the kind of case
prefaced by head or | nut of the Brazilian | variety. A little distance
quakes under its cost. Who | will fly me now? Asks | poor
Monmouth, sweltering | in the rain | of his name.

26.

During the sermon, Bennett appeared very penitent, and was observed to weep and often shake his head, which were the outward signs of his inner sorrow and contrition. The other two sat very composed, and the good effects they received from the pious discourses of the preachers was more hoped for, from their serious Meditation, than by any publick Tokens or Expressions of it. Hamlet speaks about the 'fruitful river in the eye' disingenuously, the document claims, since he knows very well that the 'dry eye bears its own

distinctive fruit

for the generality of mankind | are apt to take things on trust, than to give themselves the trouble to examine whether they be true or no. Elizabeth Bishop's 'Man–Moth', dragging his own inky cloak, and working on the assumption that the moon was a 'small hole at the top of the sky', felt compelled to investigate the situation first–hand, climbing the city's buildings nightly in an attempt to escape through it, with no success except in ascertaining ever more acutely the difficulty of his task; an act which though simple and, perhaps, futile, is not without its heroic aspect.

29.

'Because of the time needed in caring for pleached allées,' Donald
Wyman noted, 'they are but infrequently seen in American gardens,
but are frequently observed in Europe.' A pleached hornbeam hedge
about three metres high is a feature of the replanted town garden at
Rubens House, Antwerp, recreated from Rubens's painting 'The
Walk in the Garden' and from seventeenth-century engravings. In
1621, Anthony Van Dyke, Rubens's pupil, painted a portrait of Isabella
Brant as a gift to his master, basing it on Rubens's own drawing of his
wife, which passed through the hands of five

                                                    collectors

before being acquired by the British Museum in 1893, the same year
Frederick Jackson Turner presented his essay 'The Significance of
the Frontier in American History' to a special meeting of the
American Historical Association at the World's Columbian
Exposition in Chicago, Illinois. Like the Prince and Count Claudio,
the Rubens family are depicted as 'walking in a thick pleached alley'.
For all the riches he had acquired, van Dyck left little property,
having spent everything on living magnificently, more like a prince
than a painter.

30.

Leather and clay pottery often carry over traits from the wooden counterparts of previous generations. Clay pottery has also been found bearing rope-shaped protrusions, pointing to craftsmen seeking familiar shapes and processes while working with new materials. In this context, skeuomorphs exist as traits sought in other objects, either for their social desirability or psychological comforts. You might recall that the speaker of Robert Lowell's poem 'Skunk Hour' drives a 'Tudor Ford'. Tudor, as an (in itself unstable and loosely defined) architectural adjective, is often used to

describe

buildings characterised by half-timbering with black timbers cutting through larger panels of white stucco (or, more pertinently, in the Mock-Tudor style, thin boards added to the outside to mimic the functional and structural weight-bearing timbers of actual Tudor architecture). The style resembles, of course, the patterning of a skunk's fur. A sunken parterre surrounded on three sides by pleached allées of laburnum is a feature of the Queen's Garden, Kew, laid out in 1969 to complement the seventeenth-century Anglo-Dutch architecture of Kew Palace. Or, the car is Tudor as Blue Hill is blue.

DOLPHIN BLOOD

Or: chindogu backflip, taking the poem hostage like good terrorists
    can only dream of, the ouroboros fantasia to be in one side and out
the other in barely epileptic hyper-sanguine link farm in the tropics: how you
    sing the real drug that makes you happy, cruising for an off-ramp.
The extraordinary safety of my face is testament to the worms of pleasure pul
    sing like a demon in distress, in Miami they are fully human but cannot
stop. Dolphin blood is the answer – *breiten* disabled creatures of the night
    sing too far into the future, make it now and then, for whatever example
cannot be as generous as mountains can be, in the future I am rendered
    too late for a culture of sublime dead-ends to be annihilated by utopian
lament is everypony getting famous and the internet is shit. I will not let you out
    until you sing alright in pixelated piece work overtime, you reinforce that
with a stabbing motion and a spermy kiss: I am a dolphin inside all of you OK
    raise your right arm run widdershins around the broadband router in
the internet, the sky is a thousand anecdotes about me, no-one knows what
    narcissism *really* is, stuck outside the embassy in flames. I see you baby, and
the enormous caricature of slimy death you carry tucked inside your newborn
    is a moving video I like more than you, which is why I'm totally in love,
with you, and gurning like the truth in 1969. We are never getting out of
    here. Say it is, or it is: everything, the universal cop-out brandishing a hash
tag depletion semaphore to freeze on contact, poetry for everyone is doomed
    as that and so I write this for the dolphins, and the ponies, the epic bro
fist in the futilely elongated scratch-pad disaster faith, for the positive dialecticians
    and the courageous homeless, for the kind of people who walk out of the
poetry reading after giving up, we are excellent in time and make awesome
    feelings in the breast happen now, there is blood in my tomato soup, the world
that put it there is too. I make a statement to the following effect and it comes
    out of my mouth all wrong, I'm sorry for your original trauma but you
suck. You are not a dolphin. In Miami sex is cured and everything I've ever done
    is different. The attention wasted on some version of it steals silently
out of the camp in which life activates, the globe of parturition, the beautiful.

Evidence obtained by feeling is a necessary pancake, you accept this. On the
other hand that *was* a good chat–up line about E.T.; it is like one of those salvia
    divinorum dreams that someone had once and was cray. How much spit
sectioned out of worldly apparatus can you claim free speech for – this does
    appeal to a song of love and hate but not the bad kind. Things get sharper.
Like *Newsnight* I make mistakes, limbs akimbo in the militant effusive gesture
    of an idiot making sure of language, or the field of play, or the style of
anybody's sweet abstraction into them both personally and in tandem: OK Luna,
    for example. I was fully contemplating coming to see you. Your generosity
is viral and fame makes you more attractive, screaming like a fire in Carpet World
    and the metaphorical economy of body parts, each one bathed in flight or
fight antagonism with the rest. A dolphin has no tentacles, or suckers, or spits
    ink or lays in wait pretending to be an island and so I cannot be afraid of it,
island of my excellent best friend and teacher, world of my creation: the Eustachian
    tube is a narrow tube that connects the middle ear with the back of the adult
nose and is approx. 3–4cm long behind the middle ear free of mucus, enabling
    the eardrum to work and vibrate properly for bliss. We are made untimely for
it or, and what is more, made effortless by human love in free association with
    an article's definitive ident spree contagion risk of actually believing that, some
dp'd star behind the fabricated actual in danger, and the metric failsafe in com
    position flagging for it. The rest is history or won't be, the awful satiety
of knowing that or treading water at the Sealife Centre by the sea, Mike Weatherley
    gets lynched but doesn't get it or display the graphic magnanimity of a part
so harmoniously pregnant with the whole his face erupts in, and in any case
    there is a dolphin from my good friend on my wall. Perhaps you were actually
playing records; and the dancing was incredible, and I was like a twist of meat
    and we were walking on the dunes, we were a few inches high, and we were
characters in a video game projected onto the floor of someone's house. But we
    left the edge and climbed into the world, beat matching the exclusive beat
forever, the untrammelled exogamic artery in fresh prehensile absolute OK.

FROM 'ODE TO TL61P 3'

Dying will not mean wasting your life but bearing to
pass for nothing. It means not waiting for life to bear in
the past for nothing else. Whatever is nothing but next
to come, bearing is intrinsic. You learn it inside out
then disappear, or are probably outside already. But how
is outside when the difference sets to bear the nothing
there. The point is not to unlearn love, try to love nothing.
It stops too strictly infinite: attrition must be sung fuck
that: each and every loss of it will mean the edge away:
mean your life but nothing else, love for nothing gets it
true. Passion must be learned back start to end infinitely
or your life will end without you.

> The ratings cut to junk PDD–NOS ratings
> triiodothyronine parts shortages, it shall be
> you lashed naked short; a tight borrow fire
> engineering Lehman pre–junk libidinous
> prongs, solid waste TDO PID 6 ratings go
> gloat fit to fringe;
and once more to live and grow
> as one by what we never give
enough of any life for, but
> rejoin us by refusing love

to memory will fake and spin
> apart synthetic as smashed in
more readily is hard to prove,
> the answer is not right needed.

As on the missed and single way
> refusal is its own reward,
my best of you who are of me,
> and minded its eternity.

Drag her off the sofa and up the stairs. I do want to
hear that, I do want its reimbursement, I don't want to
ignore how it also says what I don't; but you begin to
know that the iron *would rather* be left on, acting on a
blind impulse to claw back *anything* to fetishize; until
finally, the flow of that progress is now and then more
or less imperceptibly interrupted by a bucket of sand,
bunking off a work–song on the bourgeois bogus fringe.
Your mother's tongue a prod of junk, her chin in a flying
cowpat. What do you mean as if you are beautiful? I
mean as if you never disappear. Will it equally prove
nothing? I can still imagine what it would be like to see
your face moving about and breathing, breaking open
with laughter, a harmless shadow on your neck, taking
your drugs with me, then mine, floating in the bathroom;
you grow up as a flower in my head; you had a moderately
big ass; you wrote pretty surrealist pornography about
your love to me; I could at least pretend to be able to
say anything to you, and believe in what I knew was the
pretence while it lasted by not credibly acknowledging
it, and you could do the same for me; but now you're
gone, and I'm the government. But really you're just away.
The music of the ice cream van is scrunching up the
hill of tar, don't be ordinarily afraid; liberals want the state
to be a way of life. But we suffered as a society from being
too optimistic, we thought the good times would last
forever. That led to the de facto socialization of credit,
rather than what I wanted at the time, and still want
now, and may yet definitely want forever, the planned
socialization of labour, so that the payout of immiseration
wound up infinitely deferred. That mistaken epic of
bad socialization is the material base for the late decon–
structive superstructure, a mind impressing limits nicely
warped but going flat. The rest of us, if you can believe

that, are best abandoned to trade our way through clinical
depression in infamous cycles on that fat roundabout
with the mat. Think of the things you bring home and
cram into your house, and all still there. What rips apart
the ironed sheet to find its messy face asleep, dreaming
of the Congolese reserves. But the private sector will
take up the slack, by genustupration of the levers of
fiscal power that operate the rack, taking up the blessed
strain of ownership from Iraq: unemployment will come
stretching down. Mahler is beautiful for being as if
infinitely resourceful in a climax; you want him for
a meaning for his life. Bush gave evil a bad name. It's
like you're still living in 1990, thinking you can have
everything you want.

FROM 'ODE TO TL61P 5'

The west Irish had nothing but tiny scraps of land with a cabin, a pig and potatoes; but Belfast and Dublin had England. Love gets saner, stained into the glass. All countries must work together toward a mutual resolution of currency imbalances, or risk war, says the governor of the Bank of England, tasked with making the genital stage of Godzilla inevitable; but he is right, it's the answer Jesus would give if pressed; the severance will yet amount to minus sweet fuck all. Your job is to be at that orgy and to experience maximum anxiety, write, and see what happens; it's not a joke to say that you learn from that, except you decline. Synergized to social fact, surplus grout of the myriad equivalents; at the source I is screaming or am; the consummated Islamabad dispatches rolled into a prolegomenon to an epigram. Smoke that shit. *Yes.* Passion swings both ways, unfixed to be enlarged, hungry for the majority of the earth. Robert's penis is a surprise. In my tent, it is more pink than I am. I am more red or purple or brown. I had guessed, startling me, but I sucked it anyway, not to go back; I think it was an excruciation to him and a probably morally significant embarrassment, because he never used it against me when I started punching his face in on the couch at my mother pissed herself on; get it back; why did I do that, smacking around with childish fists, deepening our wishes, blunting life in him and me; or smack that miniscule nameless boy who merely explained to me that my fantasy car for sale to him could be given wheels, when I wanted it to be flat and just glide? The Victorian English had their more innocent Green Zones in India, from which to perorate on the superiority of peace for trade; indiscreet to go

P

slaughtering around all over the place like the Russians via the French and in any case very likely more overheads to redemption. If sex is the price for that, be it what you may; after all sex disappears anyway.

Remembering nothing at all the right moments is difficult; so much of the rest of your time is exchanged for the lot; since poverty porn is the price of its spiritual opposite; what you get up to you pay for, come later; strikes are impossible unless you are quorate, don't be a speck and froth through the roof; Proudhon concealed that inflation is theft by being too famous about property; you are keeping it real; according to the definition of truth 'adequatio rei et intellectus', harmony depends on you being no better than a load of fucking things; there is no end to it; only at the end is the absolute ever what it is in truth; get what back; meanwhile regular people get impatient, adopt silence as compensation for their virtue in waiting for it; which I cannot do, and so am angry to think about; though I am not obliged to think about it; and I am not obliged to be angry either. 2. Compassion should be balanced and sustainable, like growth, not more balanced and more sustainable. Public sector workers will not solve your problem because they are net tax consumers, what you need is for people without any exposure to universalism to create the wealth. Wealth tastes better like that, anyhow. Less like Asian fusion. 3. The dream is finally to have no need of money of our own, like the government, but there is nothing to finalise; if you can't stymie their manipulations, you can settle for monitoring their surplus, but either way they're all the same, they leave you in the end for a *stärker Dasein*; a huge rope of blood the width of a golf bag falls out of his eye when you shoot into him, you are an heroic soldier; the kindness I have enjoyed has been more unusually beautiful from Hindoos than from Christians, and weirder; the very idea of a virgin birth is a slander against my sex; and yours too, whatever that is, whoever you are beside me; our tribute to the world is our desire, nothing else.

China is now a multilateral partner. That joke about the reference to the answer in the riddle in the reference to the answer to my life will be repeated without a pause until I laugh. Bush says *three* people were waterboarded, and hold the zeroes; our text today is *maintain physical integrity*, but a hundred times funnier, and therefore a hundred and one times funnier, billions of times funnier, and hereafter infinitely more funny because stupefying at a compound growth rate too big to fail. There is something we need to do about everything, something it is always hard to be. Career poets are part of the problem, smearing up the polish, drying out the fire; chucking shit all over the place; not being party to the solution; banking on the nodding head 'the reader' saying 'yes, that's what it's like' so as not to know what it's for, since meaning is easier that way, gaped at through the defrosted back window of the Audi, hence the spring for a neck; we all know where that shit got us: *being what we eat*. The British have become snobs. They don't *want* to be security guards always getting the night shifts at KFC illegally married to sewage technicians, subject to racist abuse which intelligent politicians learn they must not be seen on camera to regard as bigotry; the immigrants are real because they do. They say, I am more realistic than you. But at least you listen. The EU ones are the mainstream, the non–EU ones are the avant–garde.

P

The real cause of massive growth in the size of the
state was fighting major wars: the majority public
sector is the wages of justice for crushing the fascists.

Kissing softly round the true
hole cut out of sanity
the eyes I crossed out in a fantasy
shine right through;
to burn out the profounder hole
resolved to being dead
to love complaining in your head
in your soul;
our meaning is not an indulgence
or capital all our blood
distorting like a seed to bud
in vengeance;
our representatives will crush
their lungs up like a piston,
the Cheese Lenin grates his fist on
your toothbrush,
which I take for a sex toy, friction
conceptually bleeds
into agony, the fire feeds
its fiction;
the faces are all safely tucked
in balls of knotted dream,
make the mystery face scream
or get fucked;
what in either case they sing
only as they go
back to block up the thing you go
mad needing.

PYRAMID SCHEMES: READING THE SHARD

BY

LAWRENCE LEK

'CECI TUERA CELA,' PROCLAIMS CLAUDE FROLLO in Victor Hugo's *NOTRE DAME DE PARIS* – this will kill that. 'This' is the printing press that produced the book on Frollo's desk; 'that' is the gothic cathedral that embodies the archdeacon's entire world – his symbols, his beliefs, his rituals, and his city. 'Small things overcome great ones,' the technophobic priest laments. 'The book will kill the building.'

¶ For an author who lived in the midst of the Industrial Revolution, setting a novel in the Middle Ages could be seen as a romantic affectation for a more primitive era – one that was, for the majority, characterised by long periods of agricultural drudgery interspersed with periods of pestilence, religious fervour, and war. Nostalgic longing for a mythical golden age is a commonplace reaction to periods of rapid intellectual change and technological crisis, particularly for artists who are confronted with the threat of their craft's imminent obsolescence. Reflecting on the archdeacon's statement, Hugo's narrator surmises that 'human thought, in changing its form, was about to change its mode of expression.'

Contemporary media theorists would no doubt agree. In the two hundred years since Hugo's novel, the book has fragmented into streams of digitised messages and cathedrals have grown up into skyscrapers. Still, writers and architects continue to defy the relentless progress of technology by asserting authorship over their worlds.

¶ Architecture is prosthetic memory, a way for society to write without words. As such, Frollo's prophecy never came true. The book did not kill the building, for our thoughts operate through words and our bodies act in space.

In pre-literate society, these two were one and the same – political order was communicated through the language of architecture. Even today, we project archetypal patterns and linguistic concepts onto the simplest geometric forms. Crosses are two paths intersecting; circles conjure up a unified enclosure; triangles – the most basic of shapes – suggest the stability of a mountain. In this world of primitive signs, our interpretation depends entirely upon context. Icons cannot communicate in isolation; their development into language requires the invention of a structural grammar – an invisible system that dictates the placement of symbols in linear space.

From Stonehenge to the Parthenon, meaning was inscribed in three-dimensional form; rings of standing stones formed a microcosm of the universe, while Greek temple friezes were encoded with jingoistic propaganda. For centuries, the priesthood-literati controlled the influence of both written and built languages; their use of monumental civic architecture reflected their own determination to unify religion and state. From Mycenae to Greece, Rome to Byzantium, civilisations borrowed from the architectural languages of the past to bestow their own cities with the gravitas that only historical symbols can grant.

E

Gothic architecture broke with the tradition of following tradition. With the growth of increasingly complex political and social systems during the Middle Ages, the old ways of projecting power on the city were no longer adequate. Whereas symbolic architecture had previously faced outwards, gothic architecture started facing inwards, creating sanctuaries to house the collective acts of worship that the Christian faith demanded. Unlike the singular forms of platonic solids and monolithic sculpture, the resulting internal complexity of gothic architecture required an underlying logic that could dictate relationships between part and whole, between fragment and edifice.

Before the printing press, the opiate of religion was delivered through the external forms, interior environments and religious rites of each church building. As such, medieval masons were carriers of the secret codes of form and structure that were essential to the spread of Christianity throughout Europe. The need of the Church to consolidate its globalised network, and the concurrent growth of agricultural market towns, led to the medieval mania for cathedral-building, as these *free*-masons were granted the right to travel between Christianity's city-states without restrictions. In this proto-Eurozone, these architects translated their code into form, materialising society's transcendental aspirations into flying buttresses, towering spires and kaleidoscopic interiors. The cathedral was born.

Victor Hugo likened this newfound sophistication in architecture to the development of abstract poetry from logical grammar and purely descriptive words. NOTRE DAME DE PARIS (both as book and building) celebrated a society still naïve enough to believe in the promises of religion but sophisticated enough to develop a spatial language with the lyrical qualities of verse. Soon after, this swansong to feudal society would dissolve under the scientific and political revolutions that were the precursors to modernity.

¶ Hugo died just a few years before the Eiffel Tower was unveiled at the 1889 World's Fair, so we do not know how he would have reacted to it. We do, however, have the opinions of several of the leading writers of the time. In the 'Protest against the tower of Monsieur Eiffel', Guy de Maupassant, Alexandre Dumas, Charles Garnier and many others proclaimed:

> We come, we writers, painters, sculptors, architects, passionate lovers of the – up to now – intact beauty of Paris, to protest with all our strength and all our indignation, in the name of the underestimated taste of the French, in the name of the threatened French art and history, against the erection, in the very heart of our capital, of the useless and monstrous Eiffel Tower, which the malignancy of the public, often imprinted with a good sense and the spirit for justice, has already baptised with the name 'Tower of Babel'.

E

Despite the efforts of the artists to dampen Parisian civic libido, the Eiffel Tower became an overnight sensation. Deaf to the calls for good taste and sense, the people readily embraced their new symbol. This monument to the aesthetics of scientific engineering was built for a historic cause – the centenary of the French Revolution – yet it ended up being the beacon for a new age.

The public's enthusiasm for the Eiffel Tower refuted Hugo's predicted 'death of architecture'. The immersion in God that the cathedral offered was translated into an overwhelming experience of modernity for Parisian spectators. The heightened vantage point of the tower allowed the public to see Paris in its totality, exposing the extent of the metropolis for the first time. It was not just the skeletal transparency of the physical structure itself that shifted the language of power from the printed word back to the built edifice. The advent of photography allowed the Eiffel Tower to become an urban theatre – a stage upon which the public could use their cameras to preserve themselves for eternity. Like Notre Dame before it, this engagement between the collective's self-image and an architectural object made the Eiffel Tower inseparable from Parisian identity.

¶ From the beginning, city-builders intuitively grasped the need to build collective structures, and to associate these with their political and religious rituals. For early civilisations wanting to get closer to their gods, the simplest possible response was to draw upon the archetype of the triangle, and build mountains in the form of pyramids. In Mesopotamia, Java, Tenochtitlan and Giza, pyramids are the direct evidence of the primal desire to build upwards, closer to the sun, away from the base reality of earth.

The ability to impose order onto chaos governs civilisation, bestowing power upon those most able to control the minds and bodies of the masses. The concentration of people in a confined space (as is the case in walled cities and fortified towns) tends towards disorder. The pharaohs recognised this threat and took it as an opportunity to control the populace while consolidating their power. During the yearly flooding of the Nile Valley, thousands of farmers were left unoccupied for entire seasons; so the pharaoh's ministers decided to employ them to construct pyramids, an extravagant endeavour that would keep them engaged until the river subsided and sowing could begin again.

The monumental task of hauling rocks across the desert and assembling them into mountains meant that the pyramids were not simply monuments to god-kings, but also a pragmatic way for rulers to manage their own surplus labour. The real achievement of the entire enterprise is the notion of the *edifice project*; whereby a future goal, determined by the few, is achieved through the concerted efforts of the many. This is the earliest kind of science fiction: advanced engineering allows previously preposterous dreams (stone mountains in the desert) to become a reality.

E

Technological fantasy has lost none of its appeal today; once you have seen the pyramids at Giza, anything seems possible.

¶ Over the centuries, pharaohs, patrons, and property developers have learnt how to polarise public opinion about new buildings by focusing on the power of the word. We witness this trend in London today – whereas medieval masons simply named a new church after its location and patron saint, all of the city's major urban projects are named after extensive public relations campaigns intended to make buildings digestible to the public. Sometimes, the press pre-empts this process and gives the building its own nickname, as when the Swiss Re 30 St Mary Axe building became the Gherkin. At times, criticism from professional bodies is turned around and used positively – as in the case of the Shard, Renzo Piano's landmark tower in London Bridge.

In a latter-day version of the 'Protest against the tower of Monsieur Eiffel', the conservation group English Heritage claimed that the architect's design would be a 'shard of glass through the heart of historic London'. Their complaint, although well-intentioned, was a mistake – the tower's advertising team appropriated their phrase, turning 'Shard of Glass' into a branding exercise.

Naming the Shard was a masterstroke. By substituting visual associations of monumental power (the pyramid) with that of a seemingly insignificant fragment (a shard), the illusion of a building for the public was created. Its name does not operate as a simile – 'the building looks like a gherkin, so let's call it the Gherkin'. Here, the Shard is a shard – understood as such, the viewer perceives it as just a small part of a larger whole.

It is, furthermore, a Shard of Glass. Glass, the modernists believed, would liberate architecture from the darkness of masonry, into a new realm where everything would be bright, machine-like, and eternally new. Architectural theorists of the twentieth century equated glass with philosophical clarity, ignoring one of the material's fundamental properties – glass behaves with *relative* transparency: only if the light inside shines brighter than that outside are we able to see through it. During the day, the Shard's glass facade is never clear but reflective, giving it a highly inconspicuous camouflage as it reflects the sky around it. The Shard does not sparkle so much as mirror. It's barely there.

The form of the tower is distorted in other ways. While the sides of the pyramids at Giza are roughly equilateral in proportion, the Shard is six times taller than the width at its base. This exaggerated vertical taper means that its apparent height depends on your exact position from it – the Shard seems imposing from a distance, but smaller when you look up from street level. In addition, the top twenty-two of its ninety-five floors are for the uninhabitable spire – an empty skyscraper in itself, sitting on top of the observation deck, signifying nothing. Until the Conservative government's push for urban regeneration in the 1980s, London had been a low-rise city, dominated by the dome of St Paul's Cathedral. Even though the average height of the skyline has been rising steadily since then, the Shard's prominence makes it seem lonely – after all, its closest relatives are overseas.

In *DELIRIOUS NEW YORK*, Rem Koolhaas's 'retroactive manifesto for Manhattan', the architect interprets the city's skyscrapers as the manifestation of New York's collective unconscious. While these fantasies lie latent in every city, the manner of their development into specific instances of architecture varies greatly. In form and essence, the street grid and building regulations that govern Manhattan's skyscrapers make them distinct from their descendants in London. New York City law specifies that street-facing facades above a certain height must be set back to allow sunlight to fall on the streets below, resulting in the Ziggurat-like tops of its high-rise buildings; in London, rules preserving unobstructed 'viewing corridors' to St Paul's Cathedral determine the maximum extent of a building. Manhattan is a culture of compression, while London is a culture of restriction.

Paradoxically, this results in all of New York's skyscrapers looking the same, while London's all seek to be unique (geometrically speaking, the Shard is anti-Gherkin). It is the job of both marketing agencies and architects to appeal to our desire for individuality by making every building iconic. The successful advertising of property focuses on two opposite but complementary tools – the objectivity of impressive facts (1.2 million square feet; tallest building in Europe), and the quasi-spiritual qualities of the illuminated glass tower. In both cases, we are being sold a dream, a capitalist Excalibur rising up to us from the murky lake of London.

¶ If the Shard is a descendant of anything, it is not Manhattan's skyscrapers, but rather the most British of all architectures: the greenhouse. Appropriately, London's most forward-thinking contribution to the art of building comes not from architecture but from gardening. Joseph Paxton, architect of the Crystal Palace of the Great Exhibition of 1851, was earlier responsible for developing greenhouses at the landscaped gardens of Chatsworth. As chief gardener at the country estate, he had the opportunity to experiment with the structural properties and environmental effects of iron and cast plate glass. The transparency of the glasshouses he built did not have any spiritual or political message, but was simply a pragmatic way to retain heat and provide sunlight to plants. All of the elements were pre-fabricated and modular, allowing them to be produced in vast numbers and assembled into buildings of any size. For the Great Exhibition, Paxton simply created a glasshouse on a colossal scale, the horizontal predecessor of the Shard.

The Crystal Palace stood in Hyde Park during the summer of 1851, housing the Great Exhibition that presented six million Victorian tourists with the spectacle of modern engineering. 13,000 exhibitors from around the world displayed their wares, to the delight of the public who marvelled at the jacquard looms, kitchen appliances, daguerreotype photographs and flushing toilets. At the time, all was new. The building's name – the Crystal Palace – bestowed both mystical and regal importance on everything within it, and worshippers lined up to enter. The structure of society shifted – the machine was in service to the masses.

Even after the success of the Great Exhibition, architecture did not capitalise on the advances in manufacturing brought about by the industrial revolution. The theorists of the day debated what style it was most appropriate to build in – architecture was considered a dilettante's profession, an ornamental practice whose sole purpose was to dress palaces and mansions in the trappings of ancient Greece and Rome. Even when attempts at modernisation were made, as in the case of the Eiffel Tower and the Crystal Palace, the resulting works were dismissed as mere feats of engineering – projects derived from the shipbuilder's yard or garden estate and not from the gentleman's hand. It took decades for the aesthetic snobbery of the cultural elite to assimilate the culture of industrial production. Still, William Morris and others from the Arts and Crafts movement advocated a return to the handcrafted, to the unique identity that works of art and architecture supposedly had before the machine came along. Just as Victor Hugo had observed earlier, artists continued to fantasise about an Arcadian past just as they were facing an uncertain and unstoppable future.

❡ Parts of the Communist Manifesto read like an art critic's review of the Great Exhibition of 1851:

> All fixed, fast frozen relations, with their train of ancient and venerable prejudices and opinions, are swept away, all new formed ones become antiquated before they can ossify. All that is solid melts into air, all that is holy is profaned, and man is at last compelled to face with sober senses, his real conditions of life, and his relations with his kind. The need for a constantly expanding market for its products chases the bourgeoisie over the whole surface of the globe.

Karl Marx assumed that future society would not repeat the past, that political progress was a linear, causal process. Yet the agricultural and industrial revolutions had barely begun at the time of his death. With echoes of 'ceci tuera cela', Marx reluctantly embraced both *modernisation* – the socio-economic process of technological development – and *modernism*, the aesthetic and cultural responses to this experience.

Like Victor Hugo, Marx died just a few years before the Eiffel Tower was unveiled. Given his stance on social welfare, he might have welcomed it as the natural progression for an industrial culture that had already 'accomplished wonders far surpassing Egyptian pyramids, Roman aqueducts, and Gothic cathedrals'. Marx had used architectural metaphor to describe society – contending that civilisation is divided into base and superstructure. The base contains the fundamental forces and structures that make modern life possible – relationships of production, the division of labour, and property relations. In turn, the base determines the superstructure of society, which includes its culture, institutions, political structures, roles, and state. It was a perfect theory – if you based your research exclusively on the conditions of the working class in England.

Marx found chaos hard to accept; indeed, disorder is antithetical to both civilisation and architecture. Nevertheless, chaos has since emerged as a defining characteristic in a world so saturated with language that we invented the term *information*. Faced with too much information, the philosopher–mathematician Nassim Nicholas Taleb uses the combination of statistical analysis and anecdotal critique to make sense of a world governed by fundamentally turbulent networks (stock markets, ecosystems, societies). To Taleb, all systems that appear stable hide a deep-rooted volatility that makes them vulnerable to collapse – hence stock market crashes, catastrophic disasters, ruined civilisations. By contrast, natural systems grow without the imposition of a singular order over the whole; their dense network of interconnected systems makes them able to collectively respond to any threat to the system.

In *ANTIFRAGILE*, Taleb notes that steep competition among architects to gain commissions leads to them 'producing a compounded form of neomania'. Architects are forced to create structures that stand out, not just stand up. The resulting glossy modernism, cultivated *en masse* by the top-down imposition of urban planning schemes, lacks the wealth of intricate detail of networks that have grown over time. Whereas the cultures that built the cathedrals had an implicit understanding of architecture's place in the fabric of society, novelty-seeking designers are unable to replicate the rich aesthetic–economic textures that characterise the metropolis. London is robust; the Shard is fragile.

¶ Although Londoners know that the Shard is not really for *them*, it appears to have been accepted. This is not the case with the ArcelorMittal Orbit, Anish Kapoor's watchtower-sculpture in Stratford Olympic Park. The Orbit is the apotheosis of Taleb's 'compounded form of neomania', and was accordingly lambasted by critics and public alike for having no similarity to any existing archetype or form whatsoever. Although the monumental twisting crimson steel structure was likened to a modern-day Eiffel Tower by the media, its unpopularity was a failure of *terminology*, rather than of shape.

Unlike 'shard', 'orbit' operates as both verb and noun; as such, the word has no universally understood visual identity beyond an idea of centripetal movement. The complexity that Kapoor achieved was neither associative nor poetic, but existed simply in objective terms – as a feat of engineering, as an act of structural gymnastics, and as a demonstration of steel magnate Lakshmi Mittal's sponsorship. Although ostensibly a work of public art, no attempt at public engagement came from artist, mayor, or Olympic committee. As such, it remains a private object drawn from the fabric of collective enterprise. Despite being elliptical in form, the Orbit is pyramidal in essence.

Likening the base–superstructure model of Marxist theory to the Orbit or the Shard is perhaps too literal a comparison. At the very least, the Shard is pyramidal in shape. This choice of archetypal forms does succeed in absolving the tower from the historical baggage of complex associative meaning. Its designers, Renzo Piano Building Workshop, have fulfilled their mission admirably. As their tagline of 'Building Workshop' suggests, they champion rational craftsmanship and the articulate use of pristine materials above all else. This adherence to 'form follows function' was originally set out by the architectural modernist avant-garde. To them, architecture was both a reflection of modern society as well as an attempt to transform it. This mission, while admirable in itself, proved impossible to sustain over the twentieth century.

In the decades following World War II, architects were suddenly able to realise their most ambitious fantasies, on a scale hitherto unimaginable. The war had catalysed the development of manufacturing technology and international transportation routes, while creating a vacuum in which industrialised products were to be consumed. Bombed-out Europe had to be rebuilt, newly-formed nations needed capital cities, and American cities needed to grow suburbs to incorporate the automobile. With all these opportunities, the avant-garde discarded what Colin Rowe called 'that mishmash of millennialistic illusions, chiliastic excitements, and quasi-Marxist fantasies' and capitulated to the bureaucratic planning agencies that lead to the metropolis as we know it today. Architecture was purged of its ideological content, simply becoming 'a suitable veneer for the corporate activities of enlightened capitalism'. The Shard is a product of this evolution.

❡ Gestation takes a long time in architecture; the world that greets a completed skyscraper is no longer the same world that surrounded it when its foundations were cast. Propelled by the internet, the language of taste mutates at a faster rate than ever before. Images of buildings appear online years before they are built. Like website domain names, memorable shapes for buildings are difficult to come by; by the time they appear, stylistic trends have moved on.

Contemporary critics bemoan the culture of the celebrity architect, as if the media-friendly master-builder was a new phenomenon. Still, contemporary 'starchitects' like Zaha Hadid, Daniel Libeskind, Rem Koolhaas, Renzo Piano or even Anish Kapoor cannot compete with Imhotep, architect and engineer of the first pyramids at Djoser.

E

The polymath was a product of an absolutist god–monarchy. As physician, chancellor to the pharaoh and high priest of the sun god Re, his cult of personality was so strong that he was accorded divine status after death. Although we would like to think our world has moved on, society still lionises its icons. This is inevitable – after all, *everything* is drawn towards stars.

Once we have become accustomed to novelty, we demand it everywhere, including architecture. The use of the computer in three–dimensional modelling has allowed designers to produce an infinite number of complex geometric shapes. Yet despite these advances in digital clay, the number of possible forms for buildings remains limited. Faced with gravity, there are only a certain number of directions you can go – inwards (Shard), outwards (Gherkin), or around and around (Orbit). In addition, the palette of material effects is large, but finite (shiny, matte, opaque, transparent, colour, tone, hue). Lost in a sea of digital choice and formal concerns, 'starchitecture' is disconnected from the reality of built space, and from the drive towards utopia that the modernists started but did not finish.

Today, architecture arrives to us branded and packaged, so that we know of its future existence long before we perceive it in form. We no longer speak about aesthetic qualities – *how* buildings look; rather we talk about what they look *like*. The Shard suffers not from its physical structure – which is undoubtedly well-engineered – but from the same nostalgia that Hugo faced when writing *Notre Dame de Paris*. The difference is that the outdated ideal is no longer the world-in-a-building of the Middle Ages, but the world-as-a-machine of the twentieth century. Indeed, it is hard to imagine an author giving the skyscraper centre stage in a great work of fiction. In a *reductio ad absurdum* of the modernist dictum 'Less is More', the Shard cannot become any less. The building is no longer an author's novel; it is a machine's haiku.

❡ With this in mind, it is easier to identify with Hugo's nostalgia for a gothic age, an age that focused on the salvation of the collective rather than on the fulfilment of the individual. Notre Dame's anonymous masons and sculptors sought to imbue the cathedral with the infinite complexity of god's kingdom. They sought to manifest an entire cosmology within a building, and to invite people into that space as a communal experience. In keeping with that idea of the work of art as a world-in-itself, *Notre Dame de Paris* was the first novel to encompass the whole of the city – portraying gypsies and Parisian sewer rats alongside the king of France, in a manner later used by Balzac, Flaubert and Dickens. To these authors, the novel was the medium that could encapsulate the totality of human existence, just as architecture had done in the Middle Ages.

Today, the book that supposedly killed the building has in turn been rendered obsolete by the illuminated screen. Even so, archetypes will manifest in whatever

E

medium is most appropriate for their time. Arboreal, hierarchical, pyramid, fractal – all these are varieties of organisation into which disordered systems gradually coalesce. Out of these beginnings, new forms of art and language will evolve.

Like a sprawling version of Egypt's Valley of the Kings, London is covered in arcane symbols – digital signs, machine-etchings, and hieroglyphic structures, all vying for our attention and demanding to be decoded. Today, there is no single force, technology, medium, politics or religion that rules over society. Civilisation is no longer shaped into base and superstructure. It is a rhizome – an incomprehensibly thick matrix of overlapping structures, histories, effects and languages. Gone is the machine-function of urban existence; with the sheer density of information contained in the city, architecture must return to its primary function – to allow us to find our own place in space and time. To illustrate this, let us take a trip through the Shard.

The Shard is not like any other icon; it is the Rosetta Stone of London, the tower upon which all experiences of modernity are encoded. In its form, we see monumental structures from all ages; in our experience of the building, we see other civilisations reflected in us. Looking at the Shard from across London, we are Egyptian workers gazing up at the pyramids. Entering the Shard's glass canopy from London Bridge station, we are Victorian tourists experiencing the glittering wonder of the Crystal Palace. Taking the glass elevator up to the viewing platform, we are in Paris at the 1889 World's Fair, looking out from the Eiffel Tower and seeing the city from above for the first time. Stepping out onto the Shard's observation deck, eight hundred feet above the ground, we are in Manhattan, at the opening ceremony of the Empire State Building.

Architecture and language never disappear, but slowly ossify and decompose, forming a sedimentary layer on society that we call culture. The rate at which these layers accumulate is in turn determined by the unpredictable mechanisms of technology and politics, themselves subject to disorder and revolution. It is the task of successive generations to cut through this palimpsest, and to find their own way to organise the fragments into a coherent whole. Over the past century, there have been many movements in architecture – but little progress. These 'avant-garde' movements have revolved around aesthetic fashions, philosophical trends, and technological fantasies. They have been too superficial, too academic, too technical. To progress, we must create a space that can shelter the collective, not just reflect it. Architecture must not simply express novelty – it must absorb difference: difference in culture, difference in technology, difference in language, difference in dreams. The Shard is the last building of the twentieth century. The architecture of the twenty-first century has yet to be built.

E

Works

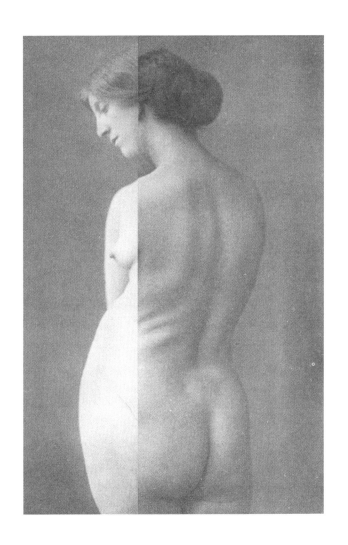

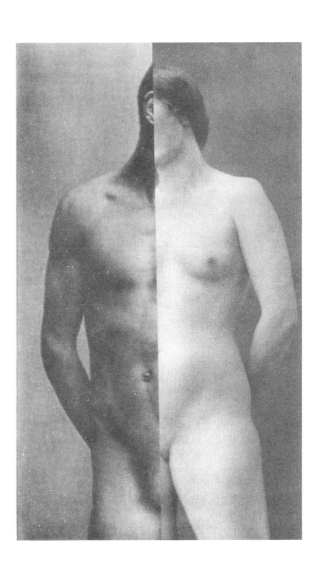

INTERVIEW

WITH

JOHN STEZAKER

JOHN STEZAKER WON THE DEUTSCHE BÖRSE PHOTOGRAPHY PRIZE FOR
HIS 2011 EXHIBITION AT THE WHITECHAPEL GALLERY. Stezaker does not, how-
ever, take photographs; he collects images, and then he cuts them up.

Stezaker has a studio in Hackney, but works mostly from his home in Kentish Town. We
talk upstairs, in his front room, which faces the street. On the walls are works he made with
copies of *FILM REVIEW* annuals. Their hard covers are primary: yellow, red and blue. He tells
me there are almost no pictures inside; he has used most of them. Stezaker has worked in collage
since the early seventies, and his most celebrated series uses film stills and portraits from the
forties and fifties. He keeps a substantial collection of these photographs downstairs: a wall of
shelves, the photographs in paper packets, stored as it came. It was purchased after the last of
several shops in Soho selling this kind of memorabilia closed down.

We look at a preliminary piece, one of an ongoing series called 'Marriage'. Two portraits,
one of a man, the other of a woman, have been slit open, the individual halves parted, and one
joined to its opposite. The new 'whole' is nonetheless made of fragments. One of the photographs
is stamped at the corner, a stain of Nationalist Socialist administration. That of Soviet East
Germany marks others. These photographs are part of a collection, which Stezaker has recently
acquired, shipped from Berlin. He estimates that it contains around 100,000 film stills and
portraits. He says it feels very alien; the photographs are 10 x 12 inches, which is not a format
he's used to working with, and the scenes are theatrical, stage-like.

Stezaker has been working on several films, one of which is connected to his German
archive, which he describes as 'an image of a supercrowd'. At the time of writing, his 'Blind'
films and accompanying collages are on show at The Approach gallery, 15 February – 17
March 2013, where he is now represented. The films are made up of stills, re-photographed and
projected, twenty-four per second. The exhibition is called *BLIND* because 'even though you're
not conscious of the image, you do of course receive it'.

Stezaker graduated from the Slade in 1973; Sigi Kraus Gallery staged his first solo show in
1970. Having emerged as one of the first wave of British Conceptual artists in the 1970s, Stezaker
worked in relative obscurity, lecturing in Contextual Studies at Central St Martins and later the
Royal College of Art before a dramatic return to prominence in the mid-2000s. In a previous
conversation I had with Stezaker he described his urge to teach, and his regret at the product of
his 'collective approach to teaching' – a committee form of consensus, a failed structure around
art education. 'In the end you have to accept that academia is not committed to success,' he said.
'It's committed to failure. It nurtures failure.' This failure is, however, essential to produce: 'It
is a background against which people do interesting things ... There are moments when ideas
electrify it [art education] and everything comes alive.'

At St Martins people used to joke about his Bs: Blanchot, Bachelard, Bataille and Barthes,
theory he taught for decades, even in the face of 'grumpy bosses' and librarians banning his
books. He often returns to these ideas in conversation. Georges Bataille describes his notion
of discontinuity in an essay titled 'Eroticism', first published in French in 1957. The dissolution
of separate beings reveals a fundamental continuity of all existence; we are individuals, who
nonetheless yearn for this 'primal continuity'. This obsession is responsible for eroticism, which
is in essence the domain of violence; the idea of death is linked with the urge to possess; the

lover would rather kill his beloved than lose her. In Stezaker's work this idea is enacted, not described, by the cut, splice, fold or tear. His works are reparative, but the image is forever mutilated by his cut; it comes back the same but different, irreversibly changed, mutated.

Stezaker embraces the conflict between saving photographs, fearing their destruction, and using them in his collage work. He describes this relationship as parasitic; if photography is the host he is its parasite, like the one that inhabits his own gut. According to French philosopher Michel Serres, parasitism operates through the logic of taking without giving. But the parasite makes exchange possible, creating connections between otherwise incommensurable forms of ordering. Before a photograph is cut, it must be separated out, the mass stored and sifted, to some extent ordered and categorised, the photographs looked at one by one. His German collection, like those already in his care, is a gift and a burden.

Q. THE WHITE REVIEW — I hear you recently acquired a new collection of photographs.

A. JOHN STEZAKER — I haven't done much research into the collection yet. It is a German archive that stretches back to the 1930s and goes up to the seventies and eighties. Rather than increasing in value, as you might expect, they seem to be plummeting. Portraits still have some kind of commercial value but ordinary film stills seem to be regarded as worthless.

Q. THE WHITE REVIEW — I wonder if that's part of the appeal to you: they are failed commodities, removed from circulation. You're rescuing them.

A. JOHN STEZAKER — For rather dubious purposes? There is a conflict between, on the one hand, saving archives that might otherwise be destroyed or dispersed, and on the other hand cutting them up, which is of course what I do.

Q. THE WHITE REVIEW — Is that necessarily a conflict?

A. JOHN STEZAKER — I feel liberated cutting something up that has been damaged or deemed worthless, but it is hypocritical; these things are historical items. The ones that are most valuable to collectors are the ones I find the least interesting; film stills tend to be produced by anonymous photographers.

It's the second collection I've rescued from probable destruction; the first archive I saved was bought specifically for my work. It contained a lot of images from the forties, fifties and sixties, which I thought I would be able to use. I discovered that, between parting with my money and collecting the archive, pretty much all of that vanished and I ended up with a substantial archive of what I would call the decline of the film still. I kept it together because it wasn't of any use to me; I can't use the material, so it's sealed. A collector told me the genre is now dead, and that there are no longer any still photographers on film sets.

Q. THE WHITE REVIEW — So the genre is dead because film stills are no longer being produced?

A. JOHN STEZAKER — Yes. This is a genre that has died, and I think we're experiencing the moment in which no one understands the value in it, least of all myself. It happens with artists' careers too; when they die there is often a moment when their work is neglected before it's rediscovered.

Q. THE WHITE REVIEW — Could you not work with digital images?

A. JOHN STEZAKER — I wouldn't need to destroy the original image to create a collage.

Q. THE WHITE REVIEW — If the image was digital there would be no relationship to sacredness and possession, no violence.

A. JOHN STEZAKER — Yes, you are quite right. There has to be a sacrifice. There is a dialectical relationship between engaging with an image and desiring its destruction. There is a consummation; what an image demands ends in a destructive act. René Girard talks about the sacrificial as being at the heart of the relationship with the image, and I think that's right. That's why I became so interested in the area of thinking that came out of Georges Bataille and continued into Maurice Blanchot. The relationship between the image and death has been a preoccupation of my teaching career, and my work. Those obsolete images are a collection of corpses; they're images that have lost their use and, to use Blanchot's term, have become 'more image', legible content.

Q. THE WHITE REVIEW — If you were teaching Bataille and Blanchot to students, how then does Bataille's notion of discontinuity, and its relationship to eroticism and violence, for example, relate to your collage work? While your collages don't demonstrate these ideas, they do have a relationship to them.

A. JOHN STEZAKER — I imagine they must do. I was giving a lecture recently, and having talked for half an hour I said, 'But I really don't know what I'm doing,' and everyone laughed. I realised that was a contradiction because I have spent a lot of time thinking about what

I do. I thought of teaching as a burden, but in retrospect it was useful to be forced every week to articulate my ideas to a hundred or so young artists. I always felt my practice was an escape from all the intellectual stuff that went on during the day, but of course it wasn't an escape at all. It never led to any enlightenment, only to a further mystery about what I'm doing, why I'm doing it, what an image is, and how I'm relating to images. Bataille's concept of continuity and discontinuity was fundamental to me; he said it is transgression that protects the taboo.

I came back from Brazil with a parasite recently, and I was thinking about how my own relationship to photography was very similar: I'm eating away at it, cutting it up, boring a little hole through this material, and yet at the same time it's about protecting it, trying to hold onto it.

Q. THE WHITE REVIEW — The parasite isn't by definition a destructive agent, and it dies with the host. If you have an analogous relationship to photographs that means you can't survive without the archival material.

A. JOHN STEZAKER — It's like the joke with the scorpion and the frog. The frog and the scorpion are drowning. Only the frog can swim so the scorpion gets onto its back. Midway the scorpion stings the frog, but just before paralysis sets in the frog asks the scorpion why he did that in the knowledge he would die too. The scorpion replies, 'It's in my nature.'

Q. THE WHITE REVIEW — Is the violent act done to the image also a recuperative, or restorative, or healing action?

A. JOHN STEZAKER — I think so. I do see my work as having a redemptive, healing function. When I look at my earliest collages I'm more aware of how violent they are. I almost don't recognise the slightly sadistic streak in the early collages, especially in relation to sexual imagery. It seems very remote to me now, but I think it was very much my Bataille phase.

Q. THE WHITE REVIEW — When you were using images of women and domestic situations, in the seventies?

A. JOHN STEZAKER — I was using cuts with regard to domestic space, male and female; a door becomes evacuated, heads are removed. The sexual narrative is very legible now. It is obviously easier to read one's earliest work, and the fact that it is rendered legible makes you think there are shortcomings. Blanchot says that, doesn't he, that the writer is the only one who can't read his own fiction? I know that applies to what I'm doing.

Q. THE WHITE REVIEW — But you're not sure if those works from the seventies are simply more legible as images, or whether they are more legible because you're distanced from them by time?

A. JOHN STEZAKER — Yes, it's the violence of *time*. When you're talking about violence you're talking about death. Time is a metaphor we use to locate a space outside our own space, and violence is a way of entering this space. It's the invasion of what Bataille would call continuity with death. God, the Other, whatever, enters into this space. What you see before you – stacks of images that have been around since the 1930s – is the stuff of history and its obliteration. We won't have this in the future. The dissolution of the film still is just a part of the digital evaporation of the image into the ether. I spend half my life working out where things are going to go. All I'm doing is moving paper around. It's clerical: paper, paper. It's a paper world that I'm conserving. All my apocalyptic fears are related to the destruction of paper; flood water coming from below, fires from above. At present I have eighty works in the museum in Tel Aviv [ONE ON ONE, at Tel-Aviv Museum of Art, Israel (2013)]. I heard that Hurricane Sandy destroyed one of my works in New York just this week.

Q. THE WHITE REVIEW — The same hurricane shut down half the city; a lot of electrical equipment was shot because of power surges, threatening the electronic archives of galleries and museums. Maybe paper is safer?

A. JOHN STEZAKER — On the other hand, maybe collecting and storing is a waste of time; we might as well play in the ruins, rip it all up and hope new figurations will emerge in the collage environment! It started in 1912. Nobody seems to have twigged to the fact that we are enjoying the centenary of modernist collage.

Q. THE WHITE REVIEW — We are?

A. JOHN STEZAKER — Picasso's 'Still Life with a Chair Cane' (1912). It was an apocalyptic moment because of the impending world war; everything was going to change. It took a long time to understand what the relationship of collage with its host might imply; it looks back and says there is no law; it's imposing a finite limit to what was formally infinite; it's evaluating the particular over the abstract, and the fragment over the universal. That very prioritisation has an apocalyptic dimension, as well as a desperate redemptive hope, which makes it very prone to nostalgia. Two people are at the back of my mind. One is Marcel Broodthaers, who's not really a collagist, and the other is Joseph Cornell, and Broodthaers got a lot of his ideas from Cornell. Cornell was looking for a way of reflecting on the origins of the image, the apocalyptic breakdown in the redundant image, the obsolete image. Collage is an apocalyptic activity.

Q. THE WHITE REVIEW — There was always a relationship between image and language in conceptual art in the late 1960s, when you were studying at the Slade.

A. JOHN STEZAKER — I was interested in conceptual art because it simplified a lot of things, which is a very American thing to do – break down things into their constituent parts – but I did feel that the result of the rise of the concept was this loss of the image. I talked to Jack Goldstein, who was my only contact with that group of artists because he showed with me at Nigel Greenwood Gallery. He had a very different relationship to the found image to the generation of appropriation artists, a much more European relationship, which was closer to this idea of the autonomy of the image.

Q. THE WHITE REVIEW — How did you work through that synthesis?

A. JOHN STEZAKER — It took a long time. A crucial moment was a trip to Italy in 1973 or '74. I was showing text and image, but even then it had become so strained they were coming apart. When I went to Italy I discovered *photo-romans* circulating in the streets, cinematic narratives in comic strip form, which I become fascinated with. These dominated my work for the next five or six years. That was really the point in which collage became my practice.

Q. THE WHITE REVIEW — Was this the start of your use of the film image as well?

A. JOHN STEZAKER — Kind of, I was using cinematic imagery, and I was also making films. In fact I was using the same rostrum camera as Michael Broodthaers, who was then making *VOYAGE ON THE NORTH SEA* in the Slade film basement. That's how I got to know him, how I got friendly with him. Broodthaers spoke very little English and my French was not that good, so there wasn't much communication between us.

Q. THE WHITE REVIEW — That makes your relationship with Broodthaers quite concrete.

A. JOHN STEZAKER — He was up against it really: he represented a combination between conceptual art and surrealism. It was a very uncomfortable relationship, and I loved that about him. He was very mysterious and strange, but it was exactly that bridge that I was interested in. In a way he was the heir of Duchamp, a slightly trampish heir. I loved him because he somehow corrected the orthodoxy; Duchamp wasn't an ideas man he was an image man, that's what Broodthaers pointed out. It was all about the madness of the idea.

I have a wonderful and embarrassing moment to tell you about. I was part of an exhibition in Brussels, and he was involved in a seminal exhibition at the same time and the British Council had put us up in the same hotel. One day we were thrown together. I was searching for *photo-romans*, and I was just about to walk out of an antiquarian bookshop when Marcel Broodthaers walked in. We said 'hi' and the usual things. It was one of those totally silent second-hand book shops – you could hear the turn of the pages – so I asked Marcel if he could ask the proprietor if he knew anywhere round here that might sell *photo-romans*. He went a deep scarlet. I thought, 'Oh god, I've made a mistake.' To ask for such a menial thing made me very embarrassed. He took a deep breath and asked the proprietor, and he did the same thing, went deep scarlet. I thought, 'Oh shit, what have I done here?' I couldn't really understand, but the outcome was that they certainly wouldn't have any *photo-romans* in there. They decided that I might find some in a place down the road and gave me the address. Off he went back to the hotel and off I went to find this other address, but I couldn't find it; all I could find was a porno shop. Then I realised it was the porno shop; in Belgium *photo-romans* are soft porn. Elsewhere in Europe they were romantic, and directed at women. In Belgium they had names like *LESBOS*.

Q. THE WHITE REVIEW —— It was very sweet of him to ask anyway.

A. JOHN STEZAKER —— I know, I know. It was very sweet. I could never communicate with him again. I was so embarrassed. Anyway, that was a completely irrelevant story. I can remember what I was showing there, it was a series called *EROS*, a series with multiple postcards.

Q. THE WHITE REVIEW —— You've described this time as the beginning of your practice.

A. JOHN STEZAKER —— I suppose it's the time when I gave up any attempt to conceptually control the image through words, apart from the conventional means of titling.

Q. THE WHITE REVIEW —— The artists you knew in London at the time, did they share those concerns?

A. JOHN STEZAKER —— No, not really. I found myself more and more isolated by my concerns at that time. I found it difficult to exhibit after showing a lot of this work, and the small critical reception it did get was negative, but I knew it was the direction I had to go in. There wasn't an alternative. I was letting go of authorial control, and I knew I was heading into dangerous territory. Surrealism was at that time about as taboo as could be. To be

directed by intuition at that time was regarded as pathetic and sad, and I was interested in all the things that were being jettisoned at that moment; the idea of the muse, the unconscious, I was discovering these things as they were becoming taboo territory. There's always a perversity to my own development, which I never feel in control of. That's why it's so perverse.

Q. THE WHITE REVIEW —— At that same time there were lots of exhibitions and journals in London about art and its relationship to social purpose, which you were involved in to an extent.

A. JOHN STEZAKER —— I was very involved for a time. I did see art as essentially subversive, but I enlarged the slightly limited political perspective into something bigger: the entire scopic regime of twentieth-century communications. My activity has become increasingly playful and less dependent on any claims of that kind, but that doesn't mean I've left them behind.

Q. THE WHITE REVIEW —— The work is liberated from social function?

A. JOHN STEZAKER —— I think I benefited from a couple of decades of relative obscurity; I could do what I liked. It wasn't done for anyone else other than myself. It allowed me to shed any pretence of social function. Equally, it allowed me to realise that these aspirations still had a place. I was trying to grapple with the reality of how the image is present or absent in our minds; I find the relationship with the screen and with the image deeply problematic. I see my work as a way to look at the enchantment of the image, but also the dystopia that it creates around it.

Q. THE WHITE REVIEW —— This seduction by the

image is the subject of the work but it's also your experience of the world too.

A. JOHN STEZAKER — It's not about *me*; I am trying to pursue what happens in the image. How that image came into being is not as relevant as what it is as a perpetual presence. Absorption gives everyone a sense that they're in contact with the world and one another, but that same image can also reveal our disconnection from the world. I'm a slave to this great archive of images I'm constantly sifting through. I have some commercial just-ification for my behaviour now that my work is selling, but what I am pursuing is what images *mean*.

I was talking to someone about a book by Michael Newman on Richard Prince [*ONE WORK* series, Afterall]. He left out the one thing that interested me most about the work at the time: the figure of the knight. It's an archetypal figure, the figure on horseback, the figure of death, but of course Jungian thinking isn't uppermost in Richard's work view. It's precisely *not* acknowledging those archetypal origins of 'the cowboy' that causes the figure to exist in a strange way; the image continues to circulate long after cowboys stop herding cows. That's what interests me in figures like that, as they cease to have a relationship to the real world they take up a purer contract with the imagination.

Q. THE WHITE REVIEW — The images you're drawn to when making your work aren't archetypes; they're performers, and yet anon-ymous. You don't believe the image because the subject is unrecognisable, and then there's a slippage, a disconnect, which is somehow realised through your method of cutting and joining.

A. JOHN STEZAKER — That's a good summa-ry of what happens. I discovered in my new collection an unassisted readymade that could make that point. I have been collecting un-assisted readymades for a while. A designer has defaced the film still in order to take a fragment, usually one head, for reproduction in a magazine. This one is in a circular format. Here the obliteration of the woman is perfect; it creates this figure of the muse or the ghost. One could look through thousands of images until you come to that. It says it all, you don't need to do anything to it.

Q. THE WHITE REVIEW — You have lots of different series that you're always working on, of which 'unassisted readymades' is one, is that right?

A. JOHN STEZAKER — I do collect certain things: images from films in which people are looking at photographs, people looking at books, reading letters, writing letters, smoking pipes, smoking cigarettes, I have a box of each of these. Hats. Hats off. Hats on.

Q. THE WHITE REVIEW — They sound like categories, ways of organising the material you collect.

A. JOHN STEZAKER — Yes, I aspire to that. But as soon as I get a collection going I've almost always got an idea for using it. It gets absorbed; it gets depleted. Others carry on forever. I've been collecting people talking on the telephone since the mid-1970s; it's my longest-standing collection. The idea for a book has been going for a long time, male and female on opposite pages. I've shown a few of them.

Q. THE WHITE REVIEW — Do you order by category or type?

A. JOHN STEZAKER — The sorting process is kind of important and kind of not. When I first got this material, my only relationship with the tsunami of images that came into my life was to start ordering it. It's a pretext for looking at them, sorting them; I had two categories, and sorted that into two categories, but now I look at them I don't know which is which. A particular collection is coming to fruition: people looking at photographs, people looking at books, reading letters, writing letters. I'm not sure of its final manifestation, but I get a sense that's what's happening. When a series occurs there are a few images, and then it drops down to what I call the seed image, the first image. All kinds of things can happen at that point. It's sifting; it's a series of alchemical movements, a kind of cleansing. Sometimes I think what you're looking for is the residue, the dirt, the negrido, the dark.

Q. THE WHITE REVIEW — You're collecting the residue that's left after the process?

A. JOHN STEZAKER — Yes, the process. At the end of it there's very little; it's sand through the fingers. I did that recently with billboards. I suddenly became aware that billboards were being superseded by acrylics and I better start collecting them. I got myself a lorry load of billboards and took them down to the studio — that was the pretext for that studio actually, to work with billboards. I started cutting them, and in the end I transported them here, and they disappeared too. I was interested in the pixels.

Q. THE WHITE REVIEW — One essential attribute of the images you use is that they are mass-produced. They are residue already, left in the wake of cinema, in the wake of politics. You seem to be less drawn to the unique image.

A. JOHN STEZAKER — It takes that multiplicity to make one. I definitely side on the fragment, but of course there's always a dialectic: a fragment can only exist in relation to a totality, otherwise it's not read as a fragment. Probably

the most profuse image in cinema history is the kiss; it stands for cinema. Yet that interests me. Anything profuse is great because there are a lot of them, and the joy of collecting is amplified. You think the kiss is a universal image, but in fact it becomes universal because it's overlooked. It's a strange image: two people locked together at the mouth. You know they're not really kissing because they're actors, and yet they *are* kissing. It's the strangeness of the interweaving between the particular and the universal. For me the work is always about a kind of fall from the universal into the particular. I feel it as a fall.

Q. THE WHITE REVIEW — That fall happens across all the images?

A. JOHN STEZAKER — That's what I see. Then I've got this image in front of me that's resistant to revealing what that is; it needs a good beating about. I may have to mutilate it. I may have to impose something on it. I may actually have to put something right over the object of central interest because I know so little about it. Someone was asking me exactly how I made a 'Marriage' piece, physically, right *here*. A critic came to interview me, just like you, and I showed them how it was done. I have this idea: I want to use a big nose on this little head, so now I have to find a point of connection, will it be through the eyebrow, the moustache, the nose, the teeth? Okay, the teeth. But then I've got the box of bits, the leftovers. I go through a series of partnerships before the marriage is established. That's how it occurs, and around 50 per cent of the time it was the bit that I was prepared to discard that becomes the important image, which is why nothing is ever thrown away.

ALICE HATTRICK, DECEMBER 2012

BRACKETING THE WORLD: WRITING POETRY THROUGH NEUROSCIENCE

BY

JAMES WILKES

THE ANECHOIC CHAMBER AT UNIVERSITY COLLEGE LONDON
HAS THE CLUTTER of a space shared by many people: styrofoam cups, defunct
pieces of equipment in the long purgatory between the days of their use and their
removal to the skip, and an accretion of still-living technical apparatus – amps,
speakers and laptops – perched on narrow shelves. The inner, soundproof room is
sparser, with a long-barrelled microphone and wedges of foam jagging out from every
wall; these severe surfaces are counterpoised by an old wingback chair that sags as
you sit in it. When the experimenter settles you and leaves, shutting the double doors
firmly behind her, a feeling of numbness grows with the silence. When the lights are
turned out, a thick skin of darkness settles.

The chamber has a wholly pragmatic function for psychologists and language
researchers, as a place to record stimuli free from contaminating noise; my visit,
however, was for a different purpose. I was poet-in-residence with the Speech
Communication Laboratory at UCL's Institute of Cognitive Neuroscience, and in June
2012 I spent an hour in the anechoic room. I had come for the silence, wanting to
experience one of the quietest places in the city, but Nadine, one of the lab members,
had said that plunging me into darkness for twenty minutes might help me to focus.
And so she shut the double doors, and as I sat in the pitch black, trying to quieten my
breathing, a world of sound flowered between my ears.

I have the recording I made inside the chamber when the twenty minutes was up.
It's a rambling monologue flecked with slip-ups, corrections and silences, as I try to
gather up more scraps of the vanishing experience I'm trying to describe, caught by
the way speech forces the silence it aims to document back into the realm of memory.
I know, because I can hear myself saying it, that I thought I heard a sound 'like sand
being thrown onto something metallic' phasing in and out in my right ear; something
like a persistent, twittering birdcall above me and to the right; and a dull sense of
pressure encroaching from the left. There were other bodily failings: stomach creaks
and gurgles, the wet crackle, 'almost a crumpling tin foil', of what I guessed were my
Eustachian tubes, and the refrains of Neil Young and Take That songs that bobbed
into my consciousness like bloated corpses.

The link between this mildly disconcerting experience and the making of poetry
is perhaps not obvious, but this unusual acoustic space also resonates with legend. Just
as the Castalian Spring at Delphi has been a mineral source for poets from Ovid and
Shakespeare to Denise Riley, for whom it gets lyricists 'gorgeous and pneumatic in
the throat', so the anechoic chamber is a kindred space, a kind of modernist cave of
the oracle. It was at Harvard's anechoic room, in the late forties or early fifties, that
John Cage heard 'one high and one low' sound: his nervous system and his circulating
blood, as the engineer supposedly told him. From this auricular experience, as
Cage suggested in his lecture 'Experimental Music', two interpretations follow: one

recognises the impossibility of subjective silence, and acknowledges the fundamental bruit that a living creature carries; the second, more contentious, demands that the composer attend to this unintended noise, and open 'the doors of music to the sounds that happen to be in the environment'. The poetry I'm interested in making also turns to an expanded environment, taking its materials from the infelicities of speech, the accidental rough music which can be found in rhyme or in puns, or equally in the phatic melodies of 'hmm' and 'err'. Unstructured noise is an important part of this: it may be obvious to say that poetry is torn between language as turbulent surface and language as vehicle of communication, but even if you let go of signification and dive into sound, meaning will bubble up again from next to nothing. People will extract sense from the most unpromising sources, and this can be the basis of a shared experience. This way of making is a tradition, too; one that presses the membrane of 'poetry' so close to those of composition, conceptual art, performance, lived speech or comedy, that with any luck they'll merge.

But stepping into the anechoic chamber evokes another movement too: a displacement of poetry into the spaces of science. This was motivated by my long-term disciplinary kleptomania, born from a sense that there must be more to poetry than the endless recycling of 'literary' models or personal experience, and that poetry can only be kept new by a piratical plundering of other disciplines. But if this act of transport is to be more than a gimmick, the scientific cargo has to crack apart the poetry that tries to carry it so completely that you start to doubt anything useful will be salvaged. Only a thoroughgoing wreckage of the idea of the poem can disperse the ghost of tedium; a spectre which should haunt anyone who's read the kind of poem that uses an fMRI scan or the idea of entropy as convenient figuration, an unexamined mass of science locked stolidly in the hold of a cast-iron personal lyric.

If the conjunction of poetry and science is to produce more than a wasted opportunity, in the sense of a meeting that changes nothing and leaves both parties mouthing platitudes about the importance of each other's work, the place to start, from the poetic side, might not be with scientific products but with processes, languages, techniques and equations; the messy, contested and uncertain couriers of knowledge. The brain scan might present itself as a rebus of truth-telling, of mind-reading – but this self-contained image is produced through a tangled web of procedures and principles, which range from the behaviour of nuclei within magnetic fields and the relationship between brain activity and blood-flow to the statistical procedures used to reduce noisy 'artefacts' and the design of the experiments themselves.

The kind of approach I'm interested in developing has grown through discussing or reading the work of friends and peers, such as Sandra Huber's residency with a sleep lab in Lausanne or James Harvey's poems exploring scientific formulae. The work that Sandra made for her residency focused on the experiment as performance, or

E

use the shape of her EEG readouts as a formal constraint for writing, whereas James, who died last year, was a biologist by training who produced fascinating pared-down forms for textual and visual poetry from a close engagement with mathematical equations or the principles of objective description.

To my mind though, one of the most conceptually complete attempts to rethink poetry with and through the life sciences has been Christian Bök's *XENOTEXT* project, which is now entering its final stages. For this, the poet designed a text which he has encrypted into a bacterium's DNA as a sequence of codons, or triplets of DNA. This sequence is then used by the bacterium to produce a viable protein which, when translated back from its amino acids to letters via Bök's encoding, forms a second meaningful poem produced in 'response'. The skill and time required to select the pairing of letters to codons, and to produce two meaningful poems through the double-translation of letter to codon, to amino-acid, to new letter, is mind-boggling. On top of this, Bök has had to teach himself the necessary molecular biochemistry and genetic engineering techniques, claiming that learning these skills was 'part of the artistic exercise'. It's impossible not to admire the poem's virtuoso feat of composition, and the project's deep engagement with the material and practice of biology to produce new forms for poetry. And yet when I saw Bök give a lecture in London in 2011, I was surprised to hear him professing the immortal value of literature: the only markers of human life that will outlast us, he said, are the indices of globally altered temperatures and permanently increased radiation levels; what if poetry could be added to that? It seems strange that that such a deeply romantic idea has survived its immersion in biology, but I suppose any engagement between poetry and science walks a tightrope between two strong gravitational forces, whirlpools formed from the expectations, values and historical inertias of the two communities which it attempts to balance.

The anechoic chamber is one of the many spaces that the Speech Communication Lab uses in the complex process of producing scientific knowledge: entering that space meant I could borrow more than language or metaphor from their work. The physical context of the soundproof room, the inbuilt mikes which recorded my voice, the principle of 'bracketing' a subject off from outside influences, to control or at least dampen environmental inputs: all of these elements have been diverted from their original scientific use and turned towards making poetry. The outcome, though, is just a few minutes of speech. The challenge that I'm addressing now is how to work with this source material, and open out its potential, through a series of procedures that I consider to be experiments (in a literary rather than a scientific sense; I mean that the outcomes are not determined in advance, and that they carry the possibility of failure.)

My first attempt started from a poem that I wrote whilst I was still in the anechoic chamber, a close translation of the sounds I'd experienced in that state of aural deprivation. The next step was suggested by Professor Sophie Scott's description

E

of the sounds from the anechoic chamber as acoustically 'dry', stripped of all the resonance and reverberations the fibreglass wedges absorb: as she put it, it's as if you're speaking in the middle of a desert. Would it be possible to give reverb back to this poem, to provide a kind of shack in the wilderness, a space conducive to its echoes? As I thought about this, I was reminded of 'I am sitting in a room', the famous minimalist work by the composer Alvin Lucier.

To make his piece, Lucier set up a feedback loop, reciting a text – which was also a description of what he was going to do – in a room, recording the result, and then replaying the tape in the same room while recording this second performance. As he repeated this process, over many iterations, in Lucier's words, 'the resonant frequencies of the room reinforce themselves so that any semblance of my speech, with perhaps the exception of rhythm, is destroyed.' What emerged instead, as Lucier puts it, were 'the natural resonant frequencies of the room articulated by speech'. And yet, knowing this is speech, and with Lucier's pacing and characteristic stammer resonating in our ears, the sense persists through the degradation, even as the sounds turn into deep bottle tones and high glass rubbings. Eventually though, a border is crossed, meaning finally shakes itself apart, and you're left with just a whistle and throb that sounds like water in the pipes, as Lucier's formants disappear into the room's.

Thinking about how to respond to such an example, on the semantic rather than the sonic level, I started making new versions of the original poem, allowing free associations to creep into the text, so it was eventually populated by mudflats, mainframes, linseeds, magnesium and finches. This was too subjective though: the point of Lucier's work is to gradually efface his choice of words, giving agency instead to the particular qualities of the space in which his voice is resonating. So I started playing with my computer's inbuilt speech–to–text converter. I would read out my text to it, and the computer would translate it, with a number of errors, into a new text, which I would read out in turn, incorporating the errors and allowing them to propagate. As I refined this technique, sometimes introducing my own deviations to add to the computer's, I returned to the original recording and started to use this as the basis for the distortions. Through the intercession of the audio recorder, my own voice sounded interestingly distant, disembodied; a found material like any other, to be treated with a mix of computer and human mishearings. I performed a version of this text at the Dana Centre in London last year.

While this particular series of poems is starting to settle into a fixed form, I'm still interested in the knotty concept of 'bracketing' that I found myself thinking about after the anechoic chamber experience. This essay's title, 'bracketing the world', comes from an article by the artist Charles Stankievech in the LEONARDO MUSIC JOURNAL, where he describes how the invention of headphones made it possible to investigate an acoustic space apparently 'inside' the head. But this phrase has a broader application too: in the sense of a temporary isolation of a subject from its environment, 'bracketing' seems crucial to any scientific project, which has to produce controlled experiment paradigms that will work in a laboratory contect. On the other hand, in the work of the Speech Communication Lab at least, there's a tension between this need to isolate and a desire to approach the real life context of speaking, which might happen under very different circumstances. I've felt such a tension too: focusing on the formless minima of half-heard, half-imagined sounds has been productive, but I worry about what I might be screening out; am I losing the wider context, the voice in the world, socialised and political? I found an arresting image of bracketing in William Derham's PHYSICO-THEOLOGY, a book published in 1713 as a 'demonstration of the being and attributes of God', but filled with experimental observations by the author and his Royal Society fellows. In a footnote to a chapter on the atmosphere, Derham writes about shutting up a sparrow and a titmouse in a 'compressing engine', otherwise known as an air pump, and watching them pant, vomit and eventually expire. The violence of the scene is striking, and a reminder of the potential damage in isolating subject from setting. And yet on the other hand, remembering the experience in the anechoic chamber, it seems that bracketing can only ever be partial, and that the vesicles we construct are always leaky, cold comfort though that may be to dead titmice. Despite the absence of external stimuli, the system roars to itself, and the noise of the body drags the world in through the vents of memory.

This is an exciting time for experimental writing. I can only speak from my own experience, but in the last five years, in London, I've seen a proliferation of popular reading series, publications, collaborations, and exchanges between different art forms. Performance writing and art writing have created more spaces where experiments can find an audience: there are regular nights in galleries like Parasol Unit and arts centres like Rich Mix, and occasionally in larger institutions like the Southbank, Serpentine, Whitechapel and Tate. The visibility of conceptual writing in the United States, where poets, anthologists and critics like Kenneth Goldsmith, Marjorie Perloff, Craig Dworkin and Vanessa Place have helped to bring the overlaps between poetry and conceptual art to wider attention, has added to a sense of possibility, and a determination that to be adequate to contemporary life, poetry needs to take up the multiple cultures and technologies that inflect that life. Take the database, for example: from a staple tool for scientific investigation, the growth of the web has turned it into a key form of contemporary culture (as Lev Manovich identified as early as 1998 in his article on 'Database as a Symbolic Form'). Mining or remixing data is now a common practice across many fields, and works such as Thomas Claburn's *I FEEL BETTER AFTER I TYPE TO YOU*, which makes poetry from the leaked internet search terms of anonymous third parties, respond to this new vernacular.

E

This is the context which informs this residency, and makes me frame it as an attempt to think seriously about what one laboratory's approach might offer to the idea of speech as material for poetry. In doing so, I've tried to make texts which are able to hold a conversation with one strain of a pervasive scientific and technological culture. Perhaps this method requires a kind of submission, and it could be argued that art approaches science in the guise of a supplicant today (a comparison of the relative number of scientists-in-residence to artists-in-residence would seem to suggest this). These questions of status don't really interest me though: it's true that the scientific research I've encountered seems complete and self-sufficient, attuned to its own networks and rhythms of grant-writing, lecturing, experiment, presentation, processing, submission, rewriting and publication – but seen from the outside, poetry probably seems self-sufficient too. Both forms have their legitimising structures, and translating material from one context to another does risk denaturing it, just as a protein might unfurl into a useless object in the wrong environment. The point about uselessness, though, is that a lack of apparent function can release other possibilities, as anyone who has admired the sculptural forms of the string surface models in a science museum will know. If the poems I make are twisted by their scientific freight, they simultaneously deform the research they are based on. Both elements are made strange, and I hope productively so.

FROM 'DESCRIBING SILENCE (6 DISTORTIONS)'

2.

So there's a sort of pheasant sounding to the, to the right

sound behind the curtains almost like a, like a sound

Like might sound sound, bouncing onto something metallic

It's very very quiet because it's there. And it's this kind of phasing in and out

And I was getting almost like a, almost like their linseed oil call, which was kind of quite

Armed against the right, a sort of creature's twittering sound or

Quite faint but it was really persistent like a sort of dawn french or something

and then I, then I heard my Subaru

And then I started a heart of gold attack and Neil young was kind of playing out my head

And that was kind of annoying and I couldn't. Stop it

And I think that was cos I remembered I heard it on the radio this morning

And that was just kinda fun plainchant time

Waiting for a hard unfold

Like that arm which is, which is irritating

3.

So there's a sort of sandpit sand to the, to the right

Sound behind the curtains almost like a sound

Like might pounds sound or um, or a pressure attack

It's, and it's very very minor because Neil's there and he's this kind of sealskin in and out

And I was getting almost like a, almost like their sealed oil call which was kind of quite

Bagpipes against the right. A sort of creature of scripture and sound

Quiet, thinking it was really persistent, like a sort of French polish of something

And then I heard my superior um

And then I started a denial of gold attack and the youngster was kind of playing in my head

And that was kind of annoying. Can you stop it?

Nothing else could I remember was very um, I heard on the radio this morning

And that was just kinda fun kind of almost like a plane tree whistling, waiting

Waiting for a hard and cold

By the arm, by the hairs which is irritating

5.

So there's a sort of a face in the sand–dunes to the right

A sound behind, a sort of like a tunnel at the slightest sound

But the soundest pound is creep-creeping down for the pressure

Like a sort of minah bird or something because neither serves that serious cleaning out

Another thing, almost like, almost like seals will call as a mark of respect

Clydebank hopes against the rights of creatures for a sense, a sensational sound

Quiet things in the persistent noise of a, a Republican polis or something

And then I heard my mother almost superior

And started at another goal there and the canisters playing in my head

And ours, at nine can use the, the stomach gurgle

Nothing else, I was very young, very kind of ahead of the radio this morning

A kind of rubbed crackle almost like a tree waiting

Waiting for a home goal line by line

By the arm, by the heritage incident at last

6.

So there's a sort of face of Monteverdi to the right

A sound behind, a sort of like a tidy up sound, the slightest sound

But the old town's discreet creeping down for the pressure

Letters should have minded lettuce there, that serious um, serious cleaning out

An almost like wax seal, almost like an eel's seal that marks the respect

Quite faint hopes against the right creature for a sense of, almost of gold

Quiet things, quit things and the persistent noise of their politicians and

And then I heard my mother almost whisper

And started another goal then the canisters playing in my head

And there is a nice clean, almost mud–track for their the off–road vehicle

And nothing else. I was very much, very kind of ahead of the radio this morning

The kind of red cattle and Mr. Petrie waiting

Waiting for her own goal line by line

By the arm by the wrecked heritage incident, at last

SPONSORS

FREE
EXHIBITION

Souzou

Outsider Art from Japan

28 March to 30 June 2013

Exhibitions at Wellcome Collection
183 Euston Road, London NW1 ⊖ Euston, Euston Square

wellcome collection

wellcomecollection.org/souzou

The free destination for the incurably curious

Still life

Easy life

The National Art Pass. Free entry to over 200 galleries and museums across the UK and half-price entry to the major exhibitions.

Buy yours today at artfund.org

Art Fund

APPENDIX

K BISWAS is a writer based in London.

YVES BONNEFOY was born in Tours, France, in 1923. A poet, translator of Shakespeare, Keats and Yeats (among others) and essayist (Rimbaud, Baudelaire, Goya, Celan...), he is Professor Emeritus of Comparative Poetics at the Collège de France. Among many prizes and honours he counts the Prix des Critiques, the Balzan Prize, the Franz Kafka Prize and the Griffin Lifetime Recognition Award.

BEVERLEY BIE BRAHIC'S translation of Yves Bonnefoy's *THE PRESENT HOUR* will be published by Seagull Books later this year. Her book *WHITE SHEETS* (CB editions) was a finalist for The Forward Prize, Best Collection 2012. *APOLLINAIRE: THE LITTLE AUTO* (CB Editions) also appeared in 2012.

MARINA CASHDAN is a culture and art writer, blogger and editor based in New York who has worked on staff and as a contributor to publications including *FRIEZE*, *ART IN AMERICA*, *ARTINFO*, *WALLPAPER* and *INTERVIEW*, as well as Phaidon's *VITAMIN P2: NEW PERSPECTIVES IN PAINTING* and various artist monographs and catalogues. From May 2009 to May 2010, she was executive editor at *MODERN PAINTERS*.

TALIA CHETRIT is an American artist photgrapher, living and working in New York. Her work has been exhibited throughout the United States and Europe.

NATALIE FERRIS is an editor and freelance writer based in London. She is the English Editor of the architecture journal *SPACE* and currently works for Enitharmon Press & Editions.

ALICE HATTRICK is a writer based in London. She co-produces *CAR*, a podcast about art and ideas. She is currently working on several collaborative projects, which include a production for The Yard theatre in Hackney Wick and a forthcoming publication about Butler's Wharf in Bermondsey. She is currently a second-year Masters' student in Critical Writing in Art and Design at the Royal College of Art. This is her third interview for *THE WHITE REVIEW*.

OLI HAZZARD'S first book, *BETWEEN TWO WINDOWS*, was published by Carcanet in 2012. He is writing his DPhil thesis on John Ashbery at Wolfson College, Oxford.

JENNIFER HODGSON is a writer, an academic researcher and UK Editor at Dalkey Archive Press. She is currently completing a Ph.D on British experimental fiction in the 1960s at Durham University which focuses on the work of Ann Quin, Christine Brooke-Rose, B. S. Johnson and Brigid Brophy. Her published writing includes literary criticism, interviews and journalism. Most recently, she contributed an afterword to The Coelacanth Press's republication of Brigid Brophy's THE KING OF A RAINY COUNTRY. She also co-edited (with Patricia Waugh) an issue of Dalkey Archive Press's REVIEW OF CONTEMPORARY FICTION on the future of British fiction in which a version of 'On the Exaggerated Reports...' will appear.

MICHAEL HOFMANN has translated the works of many writers, including Franz Kafka, Joseph Roth, and Hans Fallada. He teaches at the University of Florida in Gainesville.

LAWRENCE LEK is a speculative sculptor, installation artist and writer. Born in Frankfurt and now based in London, he imbues primal archetypes with modern technology to create immersive environments for private sanctuary and public assembly.

EDOUARD LEVÉ was born on 1 January 1965 in Neuilly-sur-Seine. A writer, photographer, and visual artist, Levé was the author of four books of writing – ŒUVRES, JOURNAL, AUTOPORTRAIT, and SUICIDE – and three books of photographs. SUICIDE, published in 2008, was his final book.

JESSE LONCRAINE completed his post-graduate study in Violence and Conflict at the School of Oriental and African Studies, University of London. Since graduating, he was worked on documentary films about War Crimes and Crimes Against Humanity in Guatemala, Colombia, Kenya, Uganda, and the Democratic Republic of Congo. He is currently working on a novella and his first collection of short stories.

JOE LUNA lives in Brighton, UK, where he curates the Hi Zero series of poetry readings and publishes HI ZERO magazine. Poems have previously appeared in SOUS LES PAVÉS, THE CAMBRIDGE LITERARY REVIEW, DAMN THE CAESARS, THE CLAUDIUS APP. and LANA TURNER. His most recent book is called ASTROTURF.

MAI-THU PERRET was born in 1976 in Geneva, where she lives and works. Her multi-disciplinary practice encompasses sculpture, painting, video and installation. Perret has created a complex oeuvre which combines radical feminist politics with literary texts, homemade crafts and twentieth century avant-garde aesthetics. Her ongoing project 'The Crystal Frontier', a fictional narrative chronicling the lives of a group of radically-minded women who turn their backs on the city and move to New Mexico to establish a feminist commune, anchors much of the artist's practice since 1999.

PETER STAMM was born in 1963, in Scherzingen, Switzerland. He is the author of the novels *AGNES*, *ON A DAY LIKE THIS*, *UNFORMED LANDSCAPE*, *SEVEN YEARS*, and the collection *IN STRANGE GARDENS AND OTHER STORIES*. His collection, *WE ARE FLYING*, is published by Granta Books in April 2013. He lives in Winterthur.

JAN STEYN is a translator from Afrikaans and French into English. He currently lives in Ithaca, New York.

KESTON SUTHERLAND is the author of *STUPEFACTION: A RADICAL ANATOMY OF PHANTOMS*, *THE STATS ON INFINITY*, *STRESS POSITION*, *HOT WHITE ANDY*, *NEOCOSIS*, *ANTIFREEZE* and other books, and of many essays about poetry, society and politics. He lives and works in Brighton, UK. *THE ODES TO TL61P* will be published by Enitharmon Press in April, and is available for pre-order now on their website.

PATRICIA WAUGH is a professor of English at Durham University. Her first book was *METAFICTION: THE THEORY AND PRACTICE OF SELF-CONSCIOUS FICTION* (1984); since then she has written numerous books and essays on modernism and postmodernism, intellectual history and aesthetics. She is currently working with scientists, medical practitioners, anthropologists and artists on two major funded research projects: a Wellcome-funded project on hearing voices and a Leverhulme – funded collaboration on tipping points, investigating radical change: how the new comes into the world. She will deliver the inaugural British Academy Annual Lecture on the Novel in 2014. A version of 'On the Exaggerated Reports...' will appear in Dalkey Archive Press's *REVIEW OF CONTEMPORARY FICTION* in April 2013.

JAMES WILKES is a poet, writer and researcher who has collaborated widely with scientists, artists and musicians to investigate topics such as brain imaging, camouflage and landscape. He is interested in speech as the material basis of poetry, and is poet-in-residence at UCL's Institute of Cognitive Neuroscience, supported by the Wellcome Trust. He has performed his work at the Liverpool Biennial, Ledbury Poetry Festival, and Lincoln Art Programme. www.renscombepress.co.uk / www.thevoxlab.org

FRIENDS OF THE WHITE REVIEW